empowerment have been introduced, stressing the need for independent thought and interdependent action. However, empowerment may mean various things to various people, ranging from true power sharing to giving people the illusion that they are in control of their own lives. Successful leaders are perceived to possess charisma yet they also delegate; they formulate compelling visions and hence may set the limits of empowerment. Is this a paradox? How far does one go in empowering and how much social influence is healthy? If empowerment should be taken as jointly formulating visions and missions, whom exactly should "jointly" include? Can these leaders cope with their anxiety and uncertainty that with broad participation their position may not be needed anymore, or with their fear of losing face (either internally or externally) when not in absolute charge? What is leadership, then, a role or a function that can be shared?

Another issue deals with the emphasis one gives to the leader as an individual, and the context in which this individual operates. Should one focus on individual qualities and characteristics or on the situation (degree of turbulence or crisis, followers, task, etc.) that enables this individual to occupy a leadership position and from that position influence others? An interesting example is the debate among historians about whether Hitler was a weak or a strong dictator (Kershaw, 1993). The intentionalists see Hitler's will as the causal factor in the nature of the Third Reich's domestic policy, foreign policy, and the policy *vis-à-vis* the Jews culminating in the Endlösung. The structuralists, while not denying that Hitler was guilty and that nothing happened of which he was not aware, locate the explanations for much that happened in the Third Reich in the existence of a power cartel between the SS/Police/SD complex, industry, the party, and the army. The goals of these parties sometimes coincided, sometimes conflicted, but at times were independent from one another. Hitler himself, being only one element in such a cartel, created the climate in which a cumulative radicalization could take place. He provided the ideological metaphors, while others tried to interpret Hitler's will and took action (subsequently sanctioned by Hitler) so as to gain his approval and, thus, power. Hitler himself tried, as much as possible, not to associate himself with negative policies or actions. Thus, the debate among historians resembles the debate within psychology (to what extent is behaviour a function of person variables and/or of situational variables), or even within the social sciences (between psychology and sociology). Applied to leadership: What makes (transformational) leaders successful—Their individual qualities? The nature of the situation in which they operate? Both? A unique match?

Issues that have caused and continue to cause questions to be raised, and that inspire new research, involve the extent to which the appearance and effectiveness of transformational leadership qualities are related to demographic and cultural variables. Do men and women differ in their (transformational) leadership style? If so, are these differences related to their biological sex or their gender identity, masculine or feminine? Or are women more change-oriented anyway since, being a minority at the upper levels of management, they have a stronger interest in changing the status quo? And if women seem to express a more transformation-oriented leadership style, as some would claim, or have demonstrated (Bass, Avolio, & Atwater, 1996), does that make them more effective than men? And what about collectivistic cultures versus individualistic ones; is a transformational leadership style encountered more often in the west (and is it also more effective), whereas dependency is more typical for collectivistic countries? If so, which changes can we expect given the trends of globalization? If no or only small differences between culturally diverse countries are found (Bass, 1997), how would that relate to views and findings on leadership in non-western countries as described by non-western scholars (e.g. Sinha, 1981)?

Other contingency variables concern the environment: Are transformational leaders most wanted and most likely to be successful in times of crisis, whereas "managers" are best suited for stabilizing and maintenance the status quo? An example that springs to mind is how the very charismatic Jan Carlzon was able to transform SAS into a profitable business, whereas years later, in a different business environment from the one in which he became CEO, he seemed to have lost his charisma and ultimately stepped down (Darmer, 1994). Or we can take the example of Jan Timmer, the former CEO of Philips, who launched Centurion, an organization-wide reorganization and revitalization programme. After several years of having lived up to his nickname of "the hurricane", he was replaced by Cor Boonstra, who is said to be a better leader for periods of relative stability. (Interesting in this example is how the leadership change was commented upon in the media; Timmer was very negatively depicted and blamed for bad management, while Boonstra was welcomed as the Messiah. Splitting, and the rhetoric which clearly helped this process, appeared to serve the function to make the leadership change legitimized in the eyes of both Philips employees and the larger environment. It came as a shock; Timmer was highly regarded and seen as a prototype of a successful change manager before the outbreak of negative publicity.)

Other contingencies concern the type of task; for example, is it complex, requiring novel perspectives, perhaps to be performed in difficult circumstances, or is the task routine and are work conditions easy? The former type of task more likely benefits from a transformational leadership style than the latter. Also, the level of management may be a relevant contingency factor, as managers in different positions in the hierarchy are faced with different levels of uncertainty and turbulence. This is not to mean that only CEOs need to be transformational; a very successful transformational leader that one of us has encountered was a first-line supervisor, who motivated his employees on the shop floor during a period of large-scale change, and who involved and empowered them in creating a new organization and making it work (Schruijer, 1992).

Can leadership really be studied independently of the co-workers? Is the quality of the leadership not expressed in the quality of the relations of the leaders

EUROPEAN JOURNAL OF WORK AND ORGANIZATIONAL PSYCHOLOGY, 1999, 8 (1), 1–8

Leadership and Organizational Change:
An Introduction

The .... on of
lead.. and,
unlik.. here
the r.. iness
lead.. the
TV-s.. come
publi.. y be
interp.. nter-
natio.. ige".
Unce.. ping
them.. ome
much.. hort-
term.. s of
lead... vide
adequ... s of
mana... are
form... nge.
The c.. , the
form... the
right t.. ....ning
leadership" (Burns, 1978), "transformational leadership" (Bass, 1985),
"visionary leadership" (Collins & Porras, 1997), "inspirational leadership"

Requests for reprints should be addressed to S.G.L. Schruijer, Work and Organization Research Centre, Tilburg University, PO Box 90153, 5000 LE Tilburg, The Netherlands; email: s.g.l.schruijer@kub.nl

(Bass, 1988), concepts which relate leadership to motivating people, formulating, co-developing, and communicating appealing visions, and effecting change. Thus, environmental turbulence has stimulated the search for new theories of leadership, a search that has resulted in a growing body of serious academic research and popular literature.

A related explanation for the increased attention to leaders and leadership involves the needs of both leaders and "those being led". People are searching for new identities to fit new circumstances and themselves; they are looking for adequate explanations as to why former ways of working do not suffice anymore; and, first and foremost, they are hoping, or at least desperately wanting to hope— hope that someone will show the way, can tell us what to expect, and lead us to a desirable future. In pursuit of these needs, omnipotence (Vansina, 1998) is often ascribed and expected from "the leader". Much more power is attributed to leaders than leaders themselves experience. On the contrary, they often complain of the lack of control they feel (Morgan, 1997). Yet, leaders also hope: They hope that, by finding and adequately implementing new management techniques, or by changing themselves in various ways, they can take control and shape their organizations in ways better suited to the ever-changing environment. Thus, they listen to those who have a promise. Management gurus seem to increase in number exponentially. The market for hope never saturates. In conjunction with omnipotence, the image of "the ideal leader" contains only positive aspects. Some leaders serve as best examples, being universally good; others need to be forgotten quickly, being universally bad. The process of splitting (Hinshelwood, 1989) serves the need and hope for the omnipotent leader who can reduce uncertainty and give sense to it. Some popular literature contains the danger of reinforcing simplistic images of leadership.

Fortunately, as mentioned earlier, a growing body of academic and action research on leadership and organizational change exists, studying how leaders create conditions under which organizations can change, how they manage the change, and motivate people by "envisioning", "empowering", and "energizing". Successful leaders appear to be able to deal with the complexity resulting from environmental turbulence. They (preferably with large segments of the organization) formulate clear visions for the future and inspire others in the process of its formulation and realization. Commitment is obtained via "co-creation", involvement, delegation, and empowerment. They express trust in the capabilities of employees, approach them with empathy, and emphasize the importance of continuous learning.

Despite the progress made in describing the behaviours and characteristics of successful leaders, as well as the context in which these are likely to be most effective, many questions and complex issues remain, which can only result in complex answers at best. One issue involves the issue of dependency. It is generally accepted that pure dependency on a leader, or blind followership, as was the case in the Jim Jones disaster, should be avoided. Instead, terms such as with his or her followers? Burns (1978) believes that the essence of trans-formational leadership resides in the interactions with the followers. These interactions are a function of two human entities, and not just one person—the leader. The relations that do develop between the leader and the follower contain a rich variety of emotions and affections that cannot just be captured in the traditional stereotypes of a victim, a willing subservant, or a smart manipulator (Oglensky, 1995). Followers have their own personal inner lives that colour their interactions with the leader. This explains the often observed ambivalence in most of these relations. People struggle with their dependency needs, trust, and desire to control something on the one hand and, on the other, they wish to be recognized. But they may also be envious of the leader, or of the attention their colleagues get, while at the same time, they seek promotion, or strive to overtake the leader. These relations cannot fully be understood without taking into account irrational and unconscious elements, which become expressed in repetitive patterns of behaviour, feelings, and distorted perceptions. Some study typical relations between the leader and a follower: "the second-in-command", "the sidekicks", "the partner", and "the group of followers" (Berg, 1998). The "second-in-command" is typified by a subordinate relationship with the leader backed up by a formal, institutional role. The "sidekicks" do not have that formal role but usually accompany the leader and perform important functions, as Dr Watson does in Sherlock Holmes stories. "Partners" distinguish themselves from the previously mentioned types by the fact that they are most often females, enabling the man to concentrate fully on his leadership tasks. In the study, "groups" appeared not that frequently but they do typify that follower relation-ship between the leader and a more or less cohesive group.

As the complexity of and the diversity in our organizations increase, little attention is given to the cognitive capabilities of the leader. Is it sufficient for the leader simply to build on and to rely on his or her experiences in organizations in order to manage successfully? Jaques (1976) claims, and provides some empirical evidence, that the requisite mental capacities to deal with the different leadership tasks, as one moves up in the systemic levels in the hierarchy, can be measured. Furthermore, the requisite mental capacity increases as the person takes on higher levels of responsibility. Although his one-factor theory is much debated, Jaques opens a very important dimension in leadership research.

As the environment becomes more turbulent, more attention is given to leadership in organizational change. New forms of organizations emerge, so to speak, every day, and even these are changed either in waves of major restructuring projects, or as self-initiated adjustments to improve the interactions with the changing environments. Leadership then becomes closely linked to the management of change and the provision of continuity to secure learning and preserve the organizational identity internally and externally. Balancing these often opposing dimensions becomes a critical task for generating sustainable growth. Can the leader provide continuity while managing change if the organization does move its managers around every two years? In other words, can continuity be provided independent of the changes of personnel in roles; leaders and co-workers? The common wisdom tells us it cannot. Yet mobility of people, especially of successful business unit managers, is at an all-time high, as if continuity is not considered relevant. Modern organizations not only create new questions; they also make us question the validity or relevance of what we have come to know about leaders in the past.

THE SPECIAL ISSUE

Several issues described previously are either directly or indirectly addressed in this special issue on Leadership and Organizational Change. Its purpose is to sketch current and new developments in research relevant to this theme. The intention has not been to deal with all questions, in all possible ways; rather, we made a selection. Its basis was an international workshop on transformational leadership we held at Tilburg University in 1997, sponsored by WORC (Work and Organizational Research Centre). The participants (in alphabetical order) were: Bernard Bass, Marije Berting, Cristina Fernandes da Costa, Jules van Dijck, George Dodge, Deanne den Hartog, Jerry Hunt, John Rijsman, Robert Roe, René Schalk, Sandra Schruijer, Boas Shamir, Peter Smith, Arndt Sorge, Tharsi Taillieu, Henk Thierry, Leopold Vansina, Reinout de Vries, and Gary Yukl. A variety of articles was submitted. The final composition of the issue reflects the variety of different perspectives and methodologies.

In the first contribution, Bernard Bass provides an overview of research done on the concepts of transformational and transactional leadership, and the effects of these two types of leadership style on followers. Contingency factors affecting these outcomes are discussed, as well as issues concerning measurement, and concerning the development of a transformational leadership style. A commentary is provided by Christian Vandenberghe.

Subsequently, Gary Yukl takes a critical look at theories of transformational leadership, focusing on conceptual, methodological, and measurement problems. He also presents a study on leadership behaviour dimensions, suggesting the existence of three factors: task-oriented behaviour, relations-oriented behaviour, and change-oriented behaviour.

Boas Shamir analyses the role of leadership and leadership theories against the background of changing organizations and changing environments. Questions he raises are for example: What type of leadership is called for in "postbureaucratic" and "boundaryless" organizations? "Weak" or "strong" leaders? And, how can leaders be both agents of change while at the same time provide a sense of safety?

John Rijsman reinterprets experiments done on role-playing and attitude change. He argues that it is not the verbal content of the role-playing which is responsible for attitude change, but (aspects of) the structural relation between leader (experimenter) and follower (subject). His results and his reinterpretation provide profound insights for leadership processes and the psychological meaning of work.

Taking the perspective of an action researcher, Leopold Vansina describes a particular phase in the transformation process of a business unit. His focus is on the general manager and the way he managed the change during that period, especially the way he related to his followers. The psychodynamic processes observed are discussed and related to earlier work on the characteristics of successful general managers. A commentary is written by the general manager of the business unit.

Reinout de Vries, Robert Roe, and Tharsi Taillieu study followers' need for leadership and the extent to which such need is related to charismatic leadership and its outcomes (such as job satisfaction and organizational commitment). Their findings show that need for leadership is positively correlated with characterizing one's leader as charismatic, and that need for leadership moderates the relationship between charismatic leadership and outcome variables. Jerry Hunt has provided us with a commentary.

Finally, we very briefly reflect on the content of the special issue.

REFERENCES

Bass, B.M. (1985). *Leadership and performance beyond expectations*. New York: Free Press.

Bass, B.M. (1988). The inspirational processes of leadership. *Journal of Management Development, 7*, 21–31.

Bass, B.M. (1997). Does the transactional/transformational leadership paradigm transcend organizational and national boundaries? *American Psychologist, 52*, 130–139.

Bass, B.M., Avolio, B.J., & Atwater, L. (1996). The transformational and transactional leadership of men and women. *International Review of Applied Psychology, 45*, 5–34.

Berg, D.N. (1998). Resurrecting the muse: Followership in organisations. In E.B. Klein, F. Gabelnick, & P. Herr (Eds.), *The psychodynamics of leadership* (pp. 27–52). Madison, CT: Psychosocial Press.

Burns, J.M. (1978). *Leadership*. New York: Harper & Row.

Collins, J.C., & Porras, J.I. (1997). *Built to last: Successful habits of visionary companies*. New York: Harper Business.

Darmer, P. (1994). SAS—Mergers in the air? In D. Adam-Smith & A. Peacock (Eds.), *Cases in organisational behaviour*. London: Pitman.

Hinshelwood, R.D. (1989). *A dictionary of Kleinian thought*. London: Free Association Books.

Jaques, E. (1976). *A general theory of bureaucracy*. London: Heinemann.

Kershaw, I. (1993). *The Nazi dictatorship: Problems and perspectives of interpretation*. London: Arnold.

Morgan, G. (1997). *Images of organization*. Thousand Oaks: Sage.

Oglensky, B.D. (1995). Socio-psychoanalytic perspectives on the subordinate. *Human Relations, 48*(9), 1029–1054.

Schruijer, S. (1992). Work redesign at the production department of a camera-plant. In S. Vickerstaff (Ed.), *Human resource management in Europe: Text and cases* (pp. 65–70). London: Chapman & Hall.

Sinha, J.B.P. (1981). *The nurturant task leader*. Atlantic Highlands, NJ: Humanities Press.

Vansina, L.S. (1998). Modellgläubigkeit und Omnipotenzfallen in der Organisationsberatung. In V. Dalheimer, E.E. Krainz, & M. Oswald (Eds.), *Change management: Auf biegen und brechen?* (pp. 195–200). Wiesbaden: Gabler.

Two Decades of Research and Development in Transformational Leadership

Bernard M. Bass

Center for Leadership Studies, State University of New York, Binghamton, USA

The interests of the organization and its members need to be aligned. Such is a task for the transformational leader. In contrast to the transactional leader who practises contingent reinforcement of followers, the transformational leader inspires, intellectually stimulates, and is individually considerate of them. Transformational leadership may be directive or participative. Requiring higher moral development, transformational leadership is recognized universally as a concept. Furthermore, contrary to earlier expectations, women leaders tend to be more transformational than their male counterparts. Although a six-factor model of transformational/transactional leadership best fits a diversity of samples according to confirmatory factor analyses, whether fewer factors are necessary remains an open question. Another important research question that has only been partially answered is why transformational leadership is more effective than transactional leadership in a wide variety of business, military, industrial, hospital, and educational circumstances.

INTRODUCTION

It has been 20 years since Burns (1978) published his seminal work introducing the concepts of transformational and transactional leadership. Whereas transformational leaders uplift the morale, motivation, and morals of their followers, transactional leaders cater to their followers' immediate self-interests. The transformational leader emphasizes what you can do for your country; the transactional leader, on what your country can do for you. A considerable amount of empirical research has been completed since then, supporting the utility of the distinction. Changes in the marketplace and workforce over the two decades have resulted in the need for leaders to become more transformational and less transactional if they were to remain effective. Leaders were encouraged to empower their followers by developing them into high involvement individuals and teams focused on quality, service, cost-effectiveness, and quantity of output

Requests for reprints should be addressed to B.M. Bass, Center for Leadership Studies, State University of New York, Binghamton, New York, 13902-6015, USA: email: bbass@binghamton.edu of production. The end of the Cold War placed a premium on the flexibility of employees, teams, and organizations. Jobs for the less skilled were automated out of existence or exported to the Third World. Those jobs that remained required better education and training.

Responsibility shifted downward in the flattening organizational hierarchy. Teams of educated professionals became commonplace. Increasingly, professionals saw themselves as colleagues rather than in superior–subordinate relationships. Transformational leadership, which fosters autonomy and challenging work, became increasingly important to followers' job satisfaction. The concept of job security and loyalty to the firm for one's entire career was disappearing. Steady pay, secure benefits, and lifetime employment were no longer guaranteed for meritorious performance. At the same time, transactional leadership alone could not provide job satisfaction.

Forty years ago in the United States, parents believed that it was most important to teach their children to respect authority, to respect the church, to respect one's government, and to avoid questioning authority. Today parents believe it is most important to teach their children to accept responsibility for their own actions, to be willing and confident in accepting challenges, and to question authority when necessary. The conforming organizational worker of the 1950s, totally dedicated to the firm, did not question authority. In the 1990s, much scepticism and cynicism has replaced the norms of unquestioning conformity of the 1950s.

In the 1950s, going beyond one's self-interests for the good of the organization was a norm of the organizational worker. That is, there was public and expressed acceptance of organizational goals, possibly filled with private reservations. There may have been a lot of expressed identification with the organization's goals and even internalization of the organization's beliefs. In today's more cynical world, such going beyond one's self-interests for the good of the organization requires aligning the individual members' interests and values with those of the organization. Trust in the leadership is required for willingness to identify with the organization and to internalize its values and the emergence in the workforce of transcendental organizational citizenship behaviour (altruism, conscientiousness, sportsmanship, courtesy, and civic virtues) (Podsakoff, MacKenzie, Moorman, & Fetter, 1990). For this, transformational leadership is needed along with corresponding changes in selection, training, development, and organizational policies.

The Full Range of Transactional and Transformational Leadership

Much has been done but more still needs to be done before we can fully understand and confidently make use of the full range of transactional and transformational leadership. Transactional leadership refers to the exchange relationship between leader and follower to meet their own self-interests. It may take the form of contingent reward in which the leader clarifies for the follower through direction or participation what the follower needs to do to be rewarded for the effort. It may take the form of active management-by-exception, in which the leader monitors the follower's performance and takes corrective action if the follower fails to meet standards. Or it may take the form of passive leadership, in which the leader practises passive managing-by-exception by waiting for problems to arise before taking corrective action or is *laissez-faire* and avoids taking any action.

Transformational leadership refers to the leader moving the follower beyond immediate self-interests through idealized influence (charisma), inspiration, intellectual stimulation, or individualized consideration. It elevates the follower's level of maturity and ideals as well as concerns for achievement, self-actualization, and the well-being of others, the organization, and society. *Idealized influence* and *inspirational leadership* are displayed when the leader envisions a desirable future, articulates how it can be reached, sets an example to be followed, sets high standards of performance, and shows determination and confidence. Followers want to identify with such leadership. *Intellectual stimulation* is displayed when the leader helps followers to become more innovative and creative. *Individualized consideration* is displayed when leaders pay attention to the developmental needs of followers and support and coach the development of their followers. The leaders delegate assignments as opportunities for growth.

The full range of leadership, as measured by the Multifactor Leadership Questionnaire (MLQ), implies that every leader displays a frequency of both the transactional and transformational factors, but each leader's profile involves more of one and less of the other. Those leaders who are more satisfying to their followers and who are more effective as leaders are more transformational and less transactional (Avolio & Bass, 1991).

The transactional and transformational rubric can be applied to teams as a whole and to organizations as a whole. Members of transformational teams care about each other, intellectually stimulate each other, inspire each other, and identify with the team's goals. Transformational teams are high-performing. Organizational policies and practices can promote employee empowerment, creative flexibility and *esprit de corps*.

In the same way, the paradigm can be extended to international relations, which can be conceived in terms of the extent emphasis is laid on principles (transformational) or power politics (transactional). When Pius XII talks about principles of morality, Joseph Stalin asks how many army divisions the Pope commands. When the United States sends American troops into harm's way in Bosnia, is it because US economic and political interests are threatened or is it to uphold principles of morality, humanitarianism, and world peace?

Recently, (Bass, 1998) I have reviewed what we know from research about how transformational leadership enhances commitment, involvement, loyalty, and performance of followers; how transactional leadership may induce more stress; how transformational leadership helps deal with stress among followers; and how contingencies in the environment, organization, task, goals, and relationships affect the utility of transactional and transformational leadership. Transactional leadership can be reasonably satisfying and effective but transformational leadership adds substantially to the impact of transactional leadership.

We have also learned about the effects of organizational culture and policies, and the effects of sex differences on transformational leadership. We have learned somewhat about how and what could be taught about the subject and how to predict which leaders are more likely to become more transactional or transformational. Research has been completed on whether rank and status are of consequence to exhibiting transformational leadership, or are as present among first-line supervisors and squad leaders as among CEOs and brigade commanders.

Going Beyond Self-actualization

The importance of transcending self-interests is something lost sight of by those who see that the ultimate in maturity of development is self-actualization. Consistent with Burns (1978), Handy (1994, p. 275) pointed out that Maslow's (1954) hierarchy of needs must be further elevated to go beyond one's self-oriented concerns:

> there [should] be a stage beyond self-realization, a stage [of] ... idealization, the pursuit of an ideal or a cause that is more than oneself. It is this extra stage that would redeem the self-centered tone of Maslow's thesis, which for all that it rings true of much of our experience, has a rather bitter aftertaste.

In 1978, Burns had handled this possible bitter aftertaste by describing the transforming leader as one who not only moved followers up on Maslow's hierarchy, but also moved them to transcend their own self-interests, presumably including their own self-realization. Williams (1994) showed that transformational leaders display more citizenship behaviours such as altruism, conscientiousness, sportsmanship, courtesy, and civic virtue, as well as imbue their subordinates with these same values.

Avolio and Bass (1991) chose to substitute for the term "charisma", in training and elsewhere, the term *idealized influence*, that is, being influential about ideals. At the highest level of morality are selfless ideal causes to which leaders and followers may dedicate themselves. Serving one's country to the best of one's abilities can be a powerful motivator.

We need to investigate the potential conflict of the would-be transformational leaders' motivation to achieve and self-actualize while focusing their efforts for the greater good for group, organization, or society. The resolution may lie in the alignment of personal principles with those of the group, organization, and society. One paradox for us may be that as we push the transformational process, particularly focusing on development of followers, we may shortchange the transcending of followers' self-interests. The transformational leader needs to do both by aligning the followers' self-interests in their own development with the interests of the group, organization, or society.

A related example concerns military officers who are faced with threats to their careers if, as they obey their code of honour, they notify authorities of unethical behaviour they observe in fellow officers. For in doing so they violate the quality of relationships they are expected to maintain with fellow officers in order to conform to a principle enunciated in the honour code. Whistle blowers in any organization often must choose as a matter of conscience between revealing unethical or illegal behaviour in others and avoiding risks to their achieving their career goals.

RELATED CONCEPTS AND MEASURES

The transactional/transformational paradigm is independent conceptually from the concepts of directive versus participative leadership, leader–member exchange (LMX), and the factor of consideration as measured by the Leader Behaviour Description Questionnaire, although empirical correlations with them may be found to some extent.

Directive and Participative Leadership

Transformational leaders can be directive or participative, authoritarian or democratic. Nelson Mandela is directive and transformational when he declares "Forget the past". He can be participative and transformational when he actively supports and involves himself in open, multiracial consultations. He can be directive and transactional when he promises blacks better housing in exchange for their votes and is participative and transactional when he reaches mutual agreements about sharing power with the white minority. The same leaders display both transformational and transactional behaviour as well as mix direction and participation.

Leader–member Exchange

Leader–member exchange (LMX) concentrates on the perceived quality of the dyadic relationship between a subordinate and his or her immediate supervisor (Graen & Scandura, 1986). Tejeda and Scandura (1994) examined the relationship among supervisors and subordinates in a health-care organization in terms of both transformational leadership and leader–member exchange. This had been preceded by attempts by Yukl (1989) to deal with LMX as transactional leadership because of LMX's reliance on exchange of rewards. However, subsequent examination of the development process in LMX by Graen and Uhl-Bien (1991) led to their reframing LMX as a transactional and a transformational leadership process. LMX unfolds in several stages in which trust, loyalty, and respect develop. In the first stage, LMX is transactional. If the last stage is reached, it is transformational.

LBDQ Consideration

Individualized consideration, as measured by the Multifactor Leadership Questionnaire (MLQ), is conceptually distinct from the Leader Behaviour Description Questionnaire (LBDQ) scale of consideration, although they are empirically correlated. Seltzer and Bass (1990) reported a correlation of 0.69. LBDQ consideration focuses on friendliness, approachability, and participative decision making; *individualized consideration* deals with concern for each follower as an individual and with the follower's development. It includes (Bass & Avolio, 1993a, p. 64): "knowing your followers' needs and raising them to more mature levels ... [and using] delegation to provide opportunities for each follower to self-actualize and to attain higher standards of moral development. Some leaders can be quite directive rather than participative in such actions."

According to data collected by Seltzer and Bass (1990), LBDQ initiation and consideration may substitute for transactional leadership, but not for trans-formational leadership. Much additional variance in effectiveness was accounted for by adding the MLQ transformational leadership scores to the LBDQ initiation and consideration scores in multiple regression equations. Furthermore, there are "highly reliable differences among the conceptions of managers, project supervisors, CEOs, military officers, principals, and other administrators in the distinctions between transactional leadership, transformational leadership, and LBDQ consideration and initiation of structure" (Bass & Avolio, 1993a, p. 65).

TRAINING, EDUCATION, AND DEVELOPMENT

Transformational and transactional leadership are affected by moral and personal development, and training and education.

Moral and Personal Development

Mature moral development is required of the transformational leader (Kuhnert & Lewis, 1987). One's parents' moral standards, and one's leadership experiences in school and extracurricular activities, forecast subsequent tendencies to be more transformational as adult leaders (Avolio, 1994). Avolio and Gibbons (1988) reported that industrial executives who were rated by their immediate subordinates as highly transformational, reported in retrospective interviews that their parents provided them with difficult challenges but also supported the nascent leaders' efforts whether or not they resulted in success (Gibbons, 1986). Similarly, transformational community leaders described childhood and adolescent experiences with caring but challenging parents who held high standards. Schools also made a difference, as did work experiences as a young adult (Avolio & Bass, 1994). The immature, self-aggrandizing *charismatic* is *pseudotransformational*. He or she may seem uplifting and responsible but on closer examination is found to be a false Messiah. Much more needs to be learned about the ethical and moral factors that distinguish the truly transformational leader from the pseudotransformational leader.

Training and Education

Intuitively, teaching and learning about how to be more or less constructive and corrective as a transactional leader should not be too difficult. More difficult is developing both the willingness and ability to be more transformational. Nevertheless, it is doable. Self-reports, incidents, and collegial ratings from the workplace have been collected from 200 executives and 500 community leaders which have validated the impact of the "Full Range of Leadership Development", a comprehensive training programme. Generally, positive results have been obtained. Follow-ups six months to two years later suggest modest improvements in transformational leadership, particularly in those transformational factors on which participants made plans to improve. These improvements tend to be accompanied by a reduction in the use of managing-by-exception (Bass & Avolio, 1990b, 1998).

Training to increase transformational leader behaviours begins with an examination of the implicit theories of ideal leadership that trainees carry around in their heads. The leadership is transformational and contingent rewarding. But why don't trainees practise more of it? Cases are reviewed to clarify the distinctions among the transformational and transactional leadership behaviours. A 360-degree assessment of these behaviours of all the trainees is provided from those back in the organization to which the trainees belong.

The trainees are helped to make plans on how to improve their profiles of behaviours and to deal with perceived obstacles to change. Assistance is provided by facilitators and fellow trainees. The trainees returns to their respective workplaces for three months to pursue their individual plans. Then, in a follow-up programme, the trainees review the success of their plans, revise them, and learn more about what they can do to be more transformational as a force for change in their organizational culture. Finally, they videotape their vision of their organization in two to five years to align the interests of their followers, themselves, and other stakeholders.

It will be possible to individualize the assessment and training programme through an available website in which the individual trainee receives follow-up suggestions over a 30-day period (http://leadership.mindgarden.com).

CONTINGENCIES

A case can be made for the universality of the concepts of transformational and transactional leadership (Bass, 1997). Although the original theory, model, and measurements emerged in the individualistic United States, it appears equally or even more applicable in the collectivist societies of Asia. Collectivist cultures provide the leaders with ready-made opportunities to become transformational leaders. Most subordinates in collectivist cultures already have respect for their leaders. Transformational leadership is more likely to be enhanced further by centrality of work in life and the high level of group orientation among followers.

The mutual obligation between the leaders and the followers facilitates the transformational leader's *individualized consideration*. Leaders in collectivist cultures already have a moral responsibility to take care of their subordinates, to help them prepare a career development plan, to attend their birthday parties, funeral ceremonies, and to counsel followers about personal problems. In turn, subordinates have a moral obligation to reciprocate with unquestioning loyalty and obedience. Indeed, transformational leadership may be far more pervasive in collectivist societies compared to the individualistic societies of the West (Jung, Sosik, & Bass, 1995).

In turn, this may help to explain the fast economic development of the East Asian "Five Dragons" along with the favouritism and corruption due to social obligations that block the healthy competitiveness of free markets. Within the East–West context, other contingent relationships need further examination. These include the organization's culture and the transformational leaders' contribution to it, gender differences, and the importance of transformational leadership when leaders face the diversity of ethnicity, race, and sex among their followers. We need to learn in what ways individualistic cultures can gain the benefits of the collectivist cultures for transformational leadership without the associated costs in creativity, individual freedom, and initiative.

Organizational Culture

For an organizational culture to become more transformational, top management must articulate the changes that are required. The message may be of a vision which needs to be shared about the style of leadership the organization wants to emphasize. Thus, if it wants to tap the expertise of its members to the fullest, it may highlight its "consultative" style of leadership. Changes, consistent with this message, are introduced in the daily practices of the organization. Desired role models of leadership begin at the top and are encouraged at each successive level below. The behaviours of top level leaders become symbols of the organization's new culture. Stories are created around the leader and mechanisms are developed to improve upward communication.

Leaders who are concerned about organizational renewal will seek to foster organizational cultures that are hospitable and conducive to creativity, problem solving, risk taking, and experimentation. First, after deliberation and con-sultation, they articulate changes that are desired. Next, the necessary changes in structure, processes, and practices are made and are widely communicated throughout the organization. Stites-Doe, Pillai, and Meindl (1994) examined the occurrence of transformational leadership and the way the organizational culture is adopted by employees. They showed that *individually considerate* leaders will participate in more acculturation activities than those who are not. Many other aspects of how the organizational culture can affect and be affected by its leadership need to be examined as well (Bass & Avolio, 1993b).

Sex Differences

Several studies have shown that women tend to be somewhat more transformational than their male counterparts and to some degree this is accompanied by greater satisfaction and rated effectiveness according to both male and female subordinates. Paradoxically, one might propose anti-feminine bias and disadvantage as a plausible explanation for finding that women are somewhat more transformational and therefore more likely to make effective leaders (Bass, Avolio, & Atwater, 1996). Women may have to be that much better leaders than their male counterparts to attain the same positions of responsibility and levels of success as men. On the other hand, some may argue that affirmative action has pushed women faster and higher than justified by their competencies. Nevertheless, the military, industry, and government may be moving in the right direction in promoting relatively large numbers of women into positions of leadership. The doors have opened wide in first-level and middle management, but a glass ceiling remains in the elevation of women to top management positions, except in a few industries such as publishing and retailing.

New, better controlled, studies are needed. The majority of the organizations studied have been dominated by males. We need studies which match or adjust for abilities predictive of success as a leader. If we can equalize such capabilities, will women still emerge as more transformational than men as leaders? We need to examine what happens when women are in a majority, such as in nursing. Gottlieb (1990) completed such a study on nursing administrators in veteran's hospitals and emerged with challenging contrary findings.

Diversity

In an unpublished paper, Del Castillo (undated) defined cultural competency as a set of skills for maintaining a process of ethical balance between individual rights and responsibilities. Cultural competency involves: (1) understanding the methods by which individuals/groups perceive the world and develop conceptual schemes; (2) understanding one's own conceptual scheme; (3) integrating other views into one's respective conceptual schemes; and (4) valuing the diversity of all conceptual schemes. He then goes on to show that it would be transformational leaders who would be better prepared to value and adapt to diversity among their followers. The transformational leader was expected to envisage a culturally competent organization, to *inspire* confidence in its achievement, to use *intellectual stimulation* to encourage new ways of dealing with the increasing diversity of their followers and to be empathetic with their followers' different needs as *individually considerate* leaders.

MEASUREMENT OF TRANSFORMATIONAL LEADERSHIP AND TRANSACTIONAL LEADERSHIP

Much empirical knowledge about transformational and transactional leadership to date has been from survey research using the Multifactor Leadership Questionnaire for which problems remain of multicollinearity of its scales, lower than desired reliability under some circumstances for active managing-by-exception, and questions about the universality of the factor structure of the model of the full range of leadership. Kelvin's admonition (originated by Camille Cavour) that "if you can't measure it, you don't know what you are talking about" drives the search for confirmation of understanding, theory and principles. Nevertheless, it was probably the Vietnam "body count" approach to evaluating the success of battles that gave rise to McNamara's Fallacy (Handy, 1994, p. 221):

> The first step is to measure whatever can be easily measured. This is OK as far as it goes. The second step is to disregard that which can't be easily measured or to give it an arbitrary quantitative value. This is artificial and misleading. The third step is to presume that what can't be measured easily really isn't important. This is blindness. The fourth step is to say that what can't be easily measured really doesn't exist. This is suicide.

Leadership is as much emotional and subjective as rational and objective in effect. We need to appreciate what the non-quantitative scholars in psycho-history, sociology and political science have to say about charisma and transformational leadership such as Caro's (1982) biography of Lyndon Johnson and Kets de Vries' (1994) psychoanalytic views of defects in *charismatic* leadership.

Issues in Measuring Transformational Leadership

By relaxing Weber's (1924/1947) criteria for what is to be considered *charismatic* (Bass, 1985), and then including it as one of the four dimensions of transformational leadership as idealized influence, much has been learned about transformational leadership as well as charisma. We have developed a better understanding of the behaviours exhibited by such leaders, key personality characteristics underlying those behaviours, their impact, and how charismatic personalities develop. We have also learned that some of the traits attributed to *charismatic* are the same for one's immediate supervisor as for the distant world-class leader. Other traits are different for immediate and distant *charismatic* leaders (Shamir, 1995).

Idealized influence. Idealized influence encompasses influence over ideology, influence over ideals, and influence over "bigger-than-life" issues. It was conceived as a substitute for the term *charismatic* for several reasons. First, *charismatic* had come to represent many meanings in the media and the public mind: celebrated, flamboyant, exciting, rabble-rousing, magnetic, and awe-inspiring. Second, charisma was too much associated with dictatorship and pseudotransformational leaders such as Huey Long, Benito Mussolini, and Adolf Hitler. Third, for researchers such as House (1995) and Conger and Kanungo (1988), *charisma* was an all-inclusive term for transformational leadership taking in *inspiration, intellectual stimulation*, and *individualized consideration*. And so, for training and some research purposes, the term *idealized influence* was substituted for the *charismatic* factor (Bass & Avolio, 1990a).

Charisma and Inspiration. In constructing the MLQ, the criterion of the principle of parsimony was violated when, for the purposes of fuller profile description, some of the items that are highly loaded and highly correlated (above 0.80) with the *charismatic* factor were formed to create a scale of *inspirational* motivation (see Bass, 1985, p. 214). This was done because it was believed that a leader could provide challenge and meaning through the use of simple words, slogans, symbols, and metaphors to generate acceptance of missions, without necessarily being charismatic. One did not have to identify with charismatic leaders to be aroused by them about the importance of a mission.

Repeated factor analyses have never supported the extraction of an inspirational factor from a charismatic factor. Yet there are separate bodies of literature for charismatic leadership and for inspirational leadership. The same leaders who are charismatic are also inspirational but different behaviours, attributions, and effects are involved. Tall people are heavier than short people but we still need separate scales of height and weight. Chapter 12 in *Bass and Stogdill's Handbook of Leadership* (Bass, 1990) divides itself into *charismatic*, *charisma-like*, and *inspirational* leadership. Not only are the behaviours, attributions, and effects different, but the relevant research literature is different. It may be that for purposes of quantitative study we should revert to a single factor encompassing charisma and inspirational leadership as Howell and Avolio (1993) did. However, McNamara's Fallacy (mentioned earlier) suggests that something may exist, such as the distinction between charisma and inspiration, without it being easy to measure. A confirmatory factor analysis for 3786 MLQ respondents suggests a good fit of the model for transformational leadership is given by three factors: *individualized consideration, intellectual stimulation* and *inspirational-idealized influence* (charisma) (Avolio, Bass, & Jung, in press).

An equally large-scale confirmatory factor analysis by Podsakoff et al. (1990) suggested that six factors of transformational leadership could be distinguished. In addition to individualized consideration and intellectual stimulation, they were able to divide the charismatic–inspirational sector into identifying and articulating a vision, providing a model and setting the example, fostering acceptance of group goals, and setting high performance expectations.

Multicollinearity.   Some factor studies such as an unpublished study of Air Force officers at Maxwell Field and a more recent study of Australian civil servants emerged with only a single factor of charisma or transformational leadership. This happens in some homogeneous samples, if short scales are used, with truncated versions of the MLQ. Nevertheless, three conceptually distinguishable factors—*charisma–inspiration, intellectual stimulation,* and *individualized consideration*—emerge in most studies either when using principal components factor analysis or when employing partial least squares (PLS) analysis (Avolio et al., in press). Since the transformational factors are substantially intercorrelated, a single transformational factor which combines them may satisfy the needs for parsimony in some research. Nevertheless, the three distinct factors instead of one transformational leadership factor remain useful when applied in training. Trainees can learn a lot about how to be more inspirational; they have a harder time authentically reinventing themselves as they already are intellectually stimulating.

It has been argued that the MLQ was measuring attributes and effects, not behaviours. None the less, most of the items of the MLQ concern behaviours. Only a few are attributions or effects. But particularly when assessing idealized influence, it is essential that some follower attributions be obtained because idealized influence involves the extraordinariness seen "in the eyes of the beholder" (Bass & Avolio, 1993a). And so two highly correlated scales are assessed: idealized influence attributes, which "make us proud to be associated with him or her", and idealized influence behaviours, which "specify the importance of being committed to our beliefs".

The multicollinearity in the factors of transformational leadership presents a statistical problem even as we cross cultures, but the factorial structure remains. Mean scores on the factors may vary and some behaviours may become inappropriate. For instance, in Japan, *contingent reward* is more implicit than explicit. Nevertheless, the overall factor structure continues to provide a meaningful framework (Bass, 1997). While idealized influence (charisma) is the largest component of variance in transformational leadership, the other components of intellectual stimulation and individualized consideration are important theoretically and practically. They involve different behaviours, attributions, and effects. The abusive, abrasive, *charismatic* leader does not exhibit the same amount of individualized consideration as does the warm, socially concerned charismatic. The knowledge, skills, and abilities which may help one become more intellectually stimulating may be unconnected to one's individualized consideration.

Issues in Measuring Transactional Leadership

one reads more than positive one but both required

Transformational leadership adds to the effectiveness of transactional leadership; transformational leadership does not substitute for transactional leadership. Empirical studies of this *augmentation* effect (e.g. Waldman, Bass, & Yammarino, 1990) support the original theoretical assumption (Bass, 1985). The best leaders are both transformational and transactional. Franklin Delano Roosevelt was a transactional politician as well as one of America's most transformational presidents (House, Spangler, & Woycke, 1991).

In the first and many subsequent factor analyses, two transactional factors emerged. These were the two facets of contingent reinforcement, *contingent reward*, which "informs me about what I should do to be rewarded", and contingent aversive reinforcement (relabelled *management-by-exception*), which "takes no action unless a problem becomes serious". In military work, Yammarino and Bass (1990) also split contingent *reward* into *promises* (e.g. "clarifies what I will get if I succeed") and *rewards* (e.g. "gives me what I want in exchange for showing my support for him/her").

Less effective than the proactive contingent reward is management-by-exception, which ranges in different situations from being slightly effective to slightly ineffective according to meta-analyses (e.g. Lowe, Kroeck, & Sivasubramaniam, 1996). Hater and Bass (1988), Hoover (1987), and Yammarino and Bass (1990) all found it factorially valid to further split management-by-exception into an *active* factor such as "arranges to know when things go wrong" and a *passive* factor such as "subscribes to the belief that if it 'ain't broken, don't fix it". These divisions were further justified by subsequent factor analyses (Avolio et al., in press). Generally, active managing-by-exception is likely to be more effective than passive managing-by-exception.

Laissez-faire leadership, the avoidance of leadership, such as "is absent when needed", and "takes no action even when problems become chronic" was strongly associated with subordinate dissatisfaction, conflict, and ineffectiveness. But, early on, it included some items which assessed the more positive *empowerment*, such as "lets me decide on matters about which I know best". Empowerment by the leader implied giving followers autonomy but giving it with reason and interest in what was delegated. Empowerment items were removed from the most recent standardized version of the MLQ.

Levels of Leadership

Before 1975, I was hard pressed to find the linkages between studies of leadership in small groups, leadership in formal organizations, and leadership of political and social movements. Now MLQ data and similar types of information can be gathered using the same concepts and full-range model across three levels of leadership (Yammarino & Bass, 1991): leadership of the small group (*micro-leadership*), leadership of the large organization (*macro-leadership*), and leadership of movements and societies (*meta-leadership*) (Nicholls, 1990). Thus, we see applications at the micro-level (Hater & Bass, 1988), at the macro-level (Yokochi, 1989), and at the meta-level (Bass, Avolio, & Goodheim, 1987) of the same model of transformational leadership. It also generalizes in concept across nationalities and language (Bass, 1997).

NEEDED FUTURE RESEARCH

Applied research in transformational leadership has been abundant. Basic research and theory have been in short supply. We have made an effort to track all published and unpublished studies and to maintain the collection of reports, theses, dissertations, and journal articles in the library at our Center for Leadership Studies. All users of the experimental MLQ 5X are asked to submit copies of their results to the Mind Garden, the publisher of the MLQ and manuals (email: mindgarden@msn.com).

On the one hand, of the 200 reports to date, a large majority reconfirm the "correlational hierarchy". The transformational factors are usually found more highly correlated with outcomes in effectiveness and satisfaction of colleagues than is contingent reward. Contingent reward is ordinarily more highly correlated with outcomes than is managing-by-exception, particularly passive managing-by-exception. Finally, *laissez-faire* leadership is almost uniformly negatively correlated with outcomes. There has been some demonstration of the contributions of transformational leadership to other criteria such as innovativeness and quality improvement. None the less, there has been relatively little basic research testing of the many models of linkages proposed by Bass (1985) to explain how transformational leadership works.

The closest to the promotion of fundamental understanding with empirical verification has come from work by Podsakoff et al. (1990), who have shown that *trust* is an important intervening construct. Theorization by Shamir, House and Arthur (1993) has connected the charismatic behaviour of the leader (which includes inspirational motivation, intellectual stimulation, and individualized consideration) with the self-concept and self-esteem needs of the follower, and Howell and Frost (1988), who, in testing House's 1976 Theory of Leadership (House, 1977), found that whereas initiation but not consideration could maintain high worker productivity when work group norms supported such productivity, only charismatic leadership could maintain high productivity in the face of conflicting low productivity norms. Recent contributions by House and Shamir (1993), and Shamir et al. (1993) have begun to "get to the bottom of things". These authors propose that transactional leaders focus on pragmatic paths to goals, whereas transformational leaders produce in their followers a higher: (1) salience of the collective identity in their self-concept; (2) sense of consistency between their self-concept and their actions on behalf of the leader and the collective; (3) level of self-esteem and a greater sense of self-worth; (4) similarity between their self-concept and their perception of the leader; (5) sense of collective efficacy; and (6) sense of "meaningfulness" in their work and lives.

By engaging follower self-concepts and arousing nonconscious motives of followers, the transformational leaders selectively arouse follower nonconscious achievement, affiliation, power motives (and other motives). These are nonconscious stable motives that have strong and enduring behavioural consequences. Such motive arousal results in increased engagement of the self, self-monitoring, and self-evaluation. The motive arousal engages the self-worth component of motivation and increases motivation on the part of followers.

Ultimately this leads to increased commitment to the mission since motive arousal results in increased self-engagement. Since the experience of self-worth and self-efficacy are contingent on goal attainment, it would be highly dissonant for the individual to resist commitment to the vision and mission of the leader. But yet to be explored are the many other ways that followers are transformed by leaders from concern for their self-interests to concern for their group, organization, or society. Self-interests are sacrificed because of: leader-inspired devotion to values and ideals embodied in the group; leader-inspired moral commitment to the group; leader-inspired identification with the group; leader-inspired calculation of the greater benefits to be gained from the group's success; and leader-inspired sense of obligations to serve the group ahead of oneself and a sense of loyalty to the group to defend its well-being and survival.

New methods need to be created for measuring transformational and transactional leadership. A new laboratory method appears promising to unravel the cause–effect relationships. Sosik, Avolio, and Kahai (1996) studied students linked by computer to a central server who were subjected to standardized transformational and transactional (contingent reward) messages both orally and via computer from trained confederate leaders who were in charge of the computerized group decision-support system. Transactional leaders generated a greater quantity of brainstorming suggestions but transformational leaders generated greater quality in the reports that were prepared.

We still need to learn a lot more about how perceptions differ between transformational and transactional leaders, dealing with what they think they ought to be doing in differing circumstances. Although the concepts of transformational and transactional leadership are found universally, much more still needs to be learned about how they are affected by the context in which the leadership occurs. Finally, much more explanation is needed about the workings of transformational leadership and how followers are moved from compliance, to identification, and to internalization of values and beliefs.

REFERENCES

Avolio, B.J. (1994). The "natural": Some antecedents to transformational leadership. *International Journal of Public Administration, 17,* 1559–1581.

Avolio, B.J., & Bass, B.M. (1991). *The full range of leadership development: Basic and advanced manuals.* Binghamton, NY: Bass, Avolio, & Associates.

Avolio, B.J., & Bass, B.M. (1994). *Evaluate the impact of transformational leadership training at individual, group, organizational and community levels.* Final report to the W.K. Kellogg Foundation, Binghamton University, Binghamton, New York.

Avolio, B.J., Bass, B.M., & Jung, D.I. (in press). Reexamining the components of transformational and transactional leadership using the Multifactor Leadership Questionnaire. *Journal of Occupational and Organizational Psychology.*

Avolio, B.J., & Gibbons, T.C. (1988). Developing transformational leaders: A lifespan approach. In J.A. Conger & R.N. Kanungo (Eds.), *Charismatic leadership: The elusive factor in organizational effectiveness* (pp. 276–308). San Francisco, CA: Jossey-Bass.

Bass, B.M. (1985). *Leadership and performance beyond expectations.* New York: Free Press.

Bass, B.M. (1990). *Bass and Stogdill's handbook of leadership: Theory, research, and applications* (3rd ed.). New York: Free Press.

Bass, B.M. (1997). Does the transactional/transformational leadership paradigm transcend organizational and national boundaries? *American Psychologist, 52,* 130–139.

Bass, B.M. (1998). *Transformational leadership: Industrial, military and educational impact.* Mahwah, NJ: Lawrence Erlbaum Associates Inc.

Bass, B.M., & Avolio, B.J. (1990a). *Manual for the Multifactor Leadership Questionnaire.* Palo Alto, CA: Consulting Psychologist Press.

Bass, B.M., & Avolio, B.J. (1990b). Training and development of transformational leadership: Looking to 1992 and beyond. *European Journal of Industrial Training, 14,* 21–27.

Bass, B.M., & Avolio, B.J. (1993a). Transformational leadership: A response to critiques. In M.M. Chemers & R. Ayman (Eds.), *Leadership theory and research: Perspectives and directions* (pp. 49–80). New York: Academic Press.

Bass, B.M., & Avolio, B.J. (1993b). Transformational leadership and organizational culture. *Public Administration Quarterly, 17,* 112–122.

Bass, B.M., & Avolio, B.J. (1998). You can drag a horse to water but you can't make it drink. *Journal of Leadership Studies, 5,* 1–17.

Bass, B.M., Avolio, B.J., & Atwater, L. (1996). The transformational and transactional leadership of men and women. *International Review of Applied Psychology, 45,* 5–34.

Bass, B.M., Avolio, B.J., & Goodheim, L. (1987). Biography and the assessment of transformational leadership at the world-class level. *Journal of Management, 13,* 7–19.

Burns, J.M. (1978). *Leadership.* New York, NY: Harper & Row.

Caro, R.A. (1982). *The years of Lyndon Johnson: The path to power.* New York: Knopf.

Conger, J.A., & Kanungo, R.A. (1988). *Charismatic leadership: The elusive factor in organization effectiveness.* San Francisco: Jossey-Bass.

Del Castillo, S. (undated). *The culturally competent transformational leader: A model for cross-cultural leadership.* Unpublished manuscript.

Gibbons, T.C. (1986). *Revisiting: The question of born vs. made: Toward a theory of development of transformational leaders.* Doctoral dissertation, Fielding Institute, Santa Barbara, CA.

Gottlieb, T.W. (1990). *Transactional and transformational leadership styles of chief and associate chief nurses in Department of Veterans' Affairs Medical Centers: A descriptive study.* Doctoral dissertation, Columbia University, DC.

Graen, G., & Scandura, R.A. (1986). Toward a psychology of dyadic organizing. In B.M. Staw & L.L. Cummings (Eds.), *Research in organizational behaviour.* Greenwich, CT: JAI Press.

Graen, G., & Uhl-Bien, M. (1991). The transformation of professionals into self-managing and partially self-designing contributors: Toward a theory of leadership making. *Journal of Management Systems, 42*, 25–39.

Handy, C. (1994). *Age of paradox.* Cambridge, MA: Harvard Business School.

Hater, J.J., & Bass, B.M. (1988). Superiors' evaluations and subordinates' perceptions of transformational and transactional leadership. *Journal of Applied Psychology, 73*(1), 695–702.

Hoover, N.R. (1987). *Transformational and transactional leadership: A test of the model.* Doctoral dissertation, University of Louisville, KY.

House, R.J. (1977). A 1976 theory of charismatic leadership. In J.G. Hunt & L.L. Larson (Eds.), *Leadership: The cutting edge.* Carbondale, IL: Southern Illinois University Press.

House, R.J. (1995). Leadership in the twenty-first century: A speculative inquiry. In A. Howard (Ed.), *The changing nature of work.* San Francisco: Jossey-Bass.

House, R.J., & Shamir, B. (1993). Toward the integration of transformational, charismatic and visionary theories. In M.M. Chemers & R. Ayman (Eds.), *Leadership theory and research: Perspectives and directions.* New York: Academic Press.

House, R.J., Spangler, W., & Woycke, J. (1991). Personality and charisma in the US Presidency: A psychological theory of leader effectiveness. *Administrative Science Quarterly, 36*, 364–396.

Howell, J.M., & Avolio, B.J. (1993). Transformational leadership, transactional leadership, locus of control, and support for innovation: Key predictors of consolidated business-unit performance. *Journal of Applied Psychology, 78*, 891–902.

Howell, J.M., & Frost, P.J. (1988). A laboratory study of charismatic leadership. *Organizational Behaviour and Human Decision Processes, 43*, 243–269.

Jung, D.I., Sosik, J.J., & Bass, B.M. (1995). Bridging leadership and cultures: A theoretical consideration of transformational leadership and collectivistic cultures. *Journal of Management Inquiry, 2*, 3–18.

Kets de Vries, M.F.R. (1994). The leadership mystique. *Academy of Management Executive, 8*, 73–92.

Kuhnert, K.W., & Lewis, P. (1987). Transactional and transformational leadership: A constructive/developmental analysis. *Academy of Management Review, 12*, 648–657.

Lowe, K., Kroeck, K.G., & Sivasubramaniam, N. (1996). Effectiveness of transformational and transactional leadership styles: A meta-analytic view. *Leadership Quarterly, 7*, 385–425.

Maslow, A.H. (1954). *Motivation and personality.* New York: Harper.

Nicholls, J. (1990). Rescuing leadership from Humpty Dumpty. *Journal of General Management, 16*, 76–90.

Podsakoff, P.M., MacKenzie, S.B., Moorman, R.H., & Fetter, R. (1990). Transformational leader behaviours and their effects on followers' trust in leader, satisfaction, and organizational citizenship behaviours. *Leadership Quarterly, 1*, 107–142.

Seltzer, J., & Bass, B.M. (1990). Transformational leadership: Beyond initiation and consideration. *Journal of Management, 16*, 693–703.

Shamir, B. (1995). Social distance and charisma: Theoretical notes and exploratory study. *Leadership Quarterly, 6*, 19–47.

Shamir, B., House, R.J., & Arthur, M.B. (1993). The motivational effects of charismatic leadership: A self-concept based theory. *Organization Science, 4*, 577–594.

Sosik, J., Avolio, B.J., & Kahai, S.S. (1996). *The impact of leadership style, anonymity, and group style on group potency and effectiveness in a group decision support system environment.* Unpublished Paper, Academy of Management, Cincinnati, OH.

Stites-Doe, S., Pillai, R., & Meindl, J.R. (1994). *Leadership style as a predictor of leaders' acculturating activity.* Unpublished Paper, Southern Academy of Management, New Orleans, LA.

Tejeda, M.J., & Scandura, T.A. (1994). *Leader–member exchange: Exchange or charisma?* Unpublished Paper, Southern Management Association, New Orleans, LA.

Waldman, D.A., Bass, B.M., & Yammarino, F.J. (1990). Adding to contingent-reward behaviour: The augmenting effect of charismatic leadership. *Group and Organizational Studies, 15,* 381–394.

Weber, M. (1947). *The theory of social and economic organizations* (T. Parsons, Trans.). New York: Free Press. (Original work published 1924)

Williams, E.S. (1994). *Tying up loose ends: The role of transformational leadership in OCBs, commitment, trust and fairness perceptions.* Unpublished Paper, Southern Management Association, New Orleans, LA.

Yammarino, F.J., & Bass, B.M. (1990). Long-term forecasting of transformational leadership and its effects among Naval officers: Some preliminary findings. In K.E. Clark & M.R. Clark (Eds.), *Measures of leadership* (pp. 151–169). West Orange, NY: Leadership Library of America.

Yammarino, F.J., & Bass, B.M. (1991). Person and situation views of leadership: A multiple levels of analysis approach. *Leadership Quarterly, 2,* 121–139.

Yokochi, N. (1989). *Leadership styles of Japanese business executives and managers: Transformational and transactional.* Doctoral dissertation. United States International University, San Diego, CA.

Yukl, G. (1989). Managerial leadership: A review of theory and research. *Journal of Management, 15,* 251–289.

Transactional vs. Transformational Leadership: Suggestions for Future Research

Christian Vandenberghe, Psychology Department,
Catholic University of Louvain,
Louvain-la-Neuve, Belgium

A Commentary on "Two Decades of Research and Development in Transformational Leadership" by B. Bass

Bernard Bass provides a useful and insightful synthesis of past research on transformational leadership. He also points to important areas where empirical work has made substantial progress, and describes the issues over which much work is still needed. My commentary addresses these issues by examining more precisely what lines of investigations might be of value for enriching our understanding of transformational leadership and for learning more about the mechanisms through which it operates.

CONSTRUCT VALIDATION AND SUBSTANTIVE RELATIONSHIPS

The Multifactor Leadership Questionnaire (MLQ) is widely used for measuring transactional and transformational leadership. As Bass summarizes, observed intercorrelations among MLQ transformational scales are quite high (cf. Lowe, Kroeck, & Sivasubramaniam, 1996). Even the three basic transformational dimensions, that is, individualized consideration, intellectual stimulation, and idealized influence (charisma), are strongly correlated with each other in most studies. Moreover, it has not been shown that they consistently differ in their relationships with a set of criterion measures. What needs to be done if one purports to validate more rigorously the construct represented by each transformational facet (although this might be done for transactional scales too) is to specify a set of distinct correlates or consequences that might be associated with each component. The identification of distinct nomological nets for each component of the model is a critical phase of construct validation (Schwab, 1980). Specifying and testing interconstruct linkages can serve to clarify the content domain covered by each transformational (or transactional) facet. Obviously, this process is just starting in the transactional/transformational leadership domain. However, if efforts were not directed to issues of construct validity, it would be difficult to refine current measurement of the model's components and to determine if current scales suffer from construct deficiency or contamination (Schwab, 1980). In other words, attention drawn towards issues of construct validity is necessary to determine if transformational leadership is multidimensional or unidimensional.

With respect to transformational leadership facets, past research provides some insights into specific linkages with key criteria. For example, intellectual stimulation might have a positive effect on burnout (cf. Seltzer, Numerof, & Bass, 1989), especially in professions already exposed to much sources of stress in their work environment (e.g. nurses, teachers). Determining the conditions under which intellectual stimulation has negative vs. positive consequences for employees could enrich our understanding of its meaning and implications. Under conditions of low stress, stimulating intellectually one's employees can result in more creativity and innovative behaviour. In contrast, under high stress, intellectual stimulation may be a source of role overload.

Similarly, it has been argued that transformational leadership acts upon subordinates' self-esteem and self-concept (Shamir, House, & Arthur, 1993). However, current definitions of transformational components suggest that it is through idealized influence (charisma) that leaders can best close the gap between the organization's mission and the individuals' self-concept. Investigators should determine which transformational component is most strongly associated with employees' sense of identity and self-esteem. Finally, individualized consideration might be related to individuals' needs for support and personal growth. Alternatively, individualized consideration could have detrimental effects in specific contexts. Recently, we collected some data using the MLQ in operating rooms (Vandenberghe & Gobert, 1996). We found that individualized consideration resulted in less satisfaction with the leader. Post-hoc interviews with some nurses from these operating units revealed that a head nurse who was individually considerate was perceived as threatening the nursing team. In fact, nurses perceived *individualized* consideration by the head nurse as a mark of favouritism and inequity.

The proposed hypothetical linkages are but a few examples of relationships of a more integrated nomological net that could be derived from theory and past research to sustain the construct validation of the transactional/transformational leadership model.

PERSONALITY ATTRIBUTES

Bass states that transformational leadership qualities are affected by individuals' childhood experiences. Further, he reports research showing that transformational leaders typically report their parents as being caring and setting challenging goals. One can push this argument further and assume that transformational leaders have distinct personality attributes that are different from those characterizing their transactional counterparts. Although this kind of research is still in its infancy, some studies have shown that transformational leaders exhibit specific personality attributes (Atwater & Yammarino, 1993; Dubinsky, Yammarino, & Jolson, 1995; Ross & Offermann, 1997). For example, Ross and Offermann (1997) demonstrated that high scores on transformational leadership were associated with a pattern of personality including high levels of pragmatism, nurturance, feminine attributes, and self-confidence, and low levels of criticalness and aggressiveness. A weakness of that study, however, is that it did not rule out the possibility that these attributes were also characteristic of transactional leadership since that component was unmeasured. So, future research should examine in a more systematic way how transformational leaders differ in their personality attributes from transactional ones and how these differences may explain subordinates' and/or unit performance.

An intriguing finding of Ross and Offermann's (1997) study is that personality attributes correlated with transformational leadership are qualities traditionally associated with females' role in our society: "a less aggressive and more nurturant leader" (Ross & Offermann, 1997, p. 1084). This picture is consistent with recent findings suggesting that female managers are more transformational than their male counterparts (Bass, Avolio, & Atwater, 1996). However, as Bass judiciously indicates, more research is needed to determine if true gender differences are responsible for current findings or whether these results can be attributed to differences in competencies between males and females (females having to strive harder and show more competencies to reach the same positions as men). Obviously, research examining the linkages between gender, personality, and transformational leadership is warranted.

TRAINING AND DEVELOPMENT

The preceding topic calls for another, important issue, that of training and development: Can one learn to be a transformational leader? To date, scant research attention has been devoted to this issue. Bass presents some general information concerning the (positive) results yielded by his "Full Range of Leadership Development" programme among a variety of managers and executives. However, more controlled and elaborated designs are needed to test the idea that transformational leadership can be learned and be associated with significant improvements in unit performance. In this regard, Barling, Weber, and Kelloway (1996) conducted a field experiment to assess the attitudinal and financial outcomes of a training session in transformational leadership within the banking industry. Using a pretest–posttest control group design, they showed that managers who received training were rated by their subordinates as being more transformational. The training programme followed by managers also significantly affected the subsequent organizational commitment of subordinates. Finally, evidence was also reported that branches in which managers followed the training session displayed better financial outcomes.

More (quasi-)experimental studies are needed to test the hypothesis that transformational leadership can be learned and that changes in transformational behaviours displayed by managers are responsible for increased unit performance. Moreover, researchers should establish if training in transformational leadership has comparatively more positive effects than training in the more traditional transactional leadership. Finally, longitudinal designs would be necessary for assessing the stability of effects and for determining the appropriate time lag required for leadership training sessions to exert their effects.

CONTEXTUAL INFLUENCES

A complex issue in studying leadership concerns its contextual influences. Bass does a good job of identifying contingencies that can affect transformational leaders' actions. As an example, he suggests that some organizational cultures are better hosts for transformational leaders than others. Bass (1996) describes data showing that organizational cultures described as transformational are viewed as doing more for improving the quality of products or services. In a similar vein, one may suggest that some organizational values are more conducive to transformational leadership. Recently, Den Hartog, Van Muijen, and Koopman (1996) demonstrated that departments with a leader described as transformational were viewed as emphasizing primarily values of support and innovation.

More basically, it might be that some contexts are propitious to the emergence of transformational leadership whereas others are not. Pawar and Eastman (1997) theorized that organizations differ in their receptivity to transformational leadership. In essence, they proposed that organizational receptivity varies from a negative to a positive pole. The positive pole refers to organizations (1) undergoing a period of change necessitating adaptation, (2) dominated by boundary-spanning units for dealing with environmental uncertainty, (3) characterized by a simple or an adhocratic organizational structure (i.e. structures facilitating the development of vision), or (4) with a clan mode of governance that creates an alignment between members' self-interests and the collective mission. These characteristics would facilitate the emergence of transformational leadership. The negative pole of organizational receptivity refers to organizations (1) focusing on efficiency, (2) with a task system dominated by technical cores (i.e. oriented towards predictability rather than management of uncertainty), (3) pertaining to the machine bureaucracy, professional, or divisional type of structure, or (4) with a market or bureaucratic rather than a clan mode of governance. These characteristics would generate a weak level of organizational receptivity to transformational leadership.

Although Pawar and Eastman's theory calls for empirical validation, its merit lies in proposing testable hypotheses regarding linkages between Bass's model and contextual variables. Our own work (Stordeur, Vandenberghe, & D'hoore, in press) suggests that professional organizations such as hospitals may indeed belong to the negative zone of organizational receptivity to transformational leadership. Hospitals are traditionally characterized by a lack of vision creation and implementation because professionals (nurses, physicians, etc.) are weakly committed to the organization. Using a sample of eight hospitals, we found that the scores on transformational scales obtained by nursing executives were unrelated to those developed at lower levels in the nursing ladder. This contradicts the so-called "falling dominoes effect", which states that transformational leadership displayed at the top level tends to be replicated at the next lower level of the hierarchy (Bass, Waldman, Avolio, & Bebb, 1987). The reason for our finding may be that hospitals are weakly receptive to transformational leadership. Additional research is needed to test the other contextual influences identified by Pawar and Eastman.

SEARCHING FOR MEDIATORS

In his final comments, Bass outlines several areas where research efforts are needed. In particular, he proposes that more work should address the mediating linkages between transformational leadership and work outcomes. Further, he identifies trust and individuals' self-concept as two constructs that are potential mediators of transformational leadership effects. However, Bass overlooks a construct that may still be a powerful mediating variable—psychological empowerment.

Thomas and Velthouse (1990) and Spreitzer (1995) define psychological empowerment as a psychological state subsuming four interrelated cognitions: meaning, competence, self-determination, and impact. Meaning refers to the perceived fit between the individual's values and beliefs, and the requirements of a work role. Competence is self-efficacy related to one's job. Self-determination is the felt autonomy in initiating actions at work. Finally, impact refers to the ability of an individual to influence the strategic, administrative, or operating outcomes at work. One may hypothesize that some transformational leadership facets act through empowerment in influencing work outcomes. For example, charisma may provide a sense of meaning which in turn could enhance organizational commitment. Intellectual stimulation should influence subordinates' felt competence and lead to higher in-role performance. Individualized consideration may foster self-determination and impact and indirectly result in more intrinsic job satisfaction. Additional hypotheses concerning potential mediating linkages between transformational leader behaviours and organizationally relevant outcomes could be formulated and empirically tested.

CONCLUSION

Bernard Bass's article offers a good synthesis of what we have learned and what remains to be learned about the transformational leadership workings. However, progress will be achieved only if theory building efforts lead to precise hypotheses to be tested. In this commentary, I focused on five areas of needed research: (1) construct validation (the linkage between a construct and its measurement), (2) personality attributes of transactional and transformational leaders, (3) effects of training in transformational skills on organizational outcomes, (4) contextual influences, and (5) the search for mediators.

REFERENCES

Atwater, L.E., & Yammarino, F.J. (1993). Personal attributes as predictors of superiors' and subordinates' perceptions of military academy leadership. *Human Relations, 46*, 645–668.

Barling, J., Weber, T., & Kelloway, E.K. (1996). Effects of transformational leadership training on attitudinal and financial outcomes: A field experiment. *Journal of Applied Psychology, 81*, 827–832.

Bass, B.M. (1996). *A new paradigm of leadership: An inquiry into transformational leadership.* Alexandria, VA: US Army Research Institute for the Behavioral and Social Sciences.

Bass, B.M., Avolio, B.J., & Atwater, L. (1996). The transformational and transactional leadership of men and women. *Applied Psychology: An International Review, 45*, 5–34.

Bass, B.M., Waldman, D.A., Avolio, B.J., & Bebb, M. (1987). Transformational leadership and the falling dominoes effect. *Group and Organization Studies, 12*, 73–87.

Den Hartog, D.N., Van Muijen, J.J., & Koopman, P.L. (1996). Linking transformational leadership and organizational culture. *Journal of Leadership Studies, 3*, 68–83.

Dubinsky, A.J., Yammarino, F.J., & Jolson, M.A. (1995). An examination of linkages between personal characteristics and dimensions of transformational leadership. *Journal of Business and Psychology, 9*, 315–335.

Lowe, K.B., Kroeck, K.G., & Sivasubramaniam, N. (1996). Effectiveness correlates of transformational and transactional leadership: A meta-analytic review of the MLQ literature. *Leadership Quarterly, 7*, 385–425.

Pawar, B.S., & Eastman, K.K. (1997). The nature and implications of contextual influences on transformational leadership: A conceptual examination. *Academy of Management Review, 22*, 80–109.

Ross, S.M., & Offermann, L.R. (1997). Transformational leaders: Measurement of personality attributes and work group performance. *Personality and Social Psychology Bulletin, 23*, 1078–1086.

Schwab, D.P. (1980). Construct validity in organizational research. *Research in Organizational Behavior, 2*, 3–43.

Seltzer, J., Numerof, R.E., & Bass, B.M. (1989). Transformational leadership: Is it a source of more burnout and stress? *Journal of Health and Human Resources Administration, 12*, 174–185.

Shamir, B., House, R.J., & Arthur, M.B. (1993). The motivational effects of charismatic leadership: A self-concept based theory. *Organization Science, 4*, 577–594.

Spreitzer, G.M. (1995). Psychological empowerment in the workplace: Dimensions, measurement, and validation. *Academy of Management Journal, 38*, 1442–1465.

Stordeur, S., Vandenberghe, C., & D'hoore, W. (in press). Leadership styles across hierarchical levels in nursing departments. *Nursing Research*.

Thomas, K.W., & Velthouse, B.A. (1990). Cognitive elements of empowerment. *Academy of Management Review, 15*, 666–681.

Vandenberghe, C., & Gobert, P. (1996). *Transformational leadership, transactional leadership, job scope, and culture in nursing subunits: How they relate to work outcomes.* Unpublished manuscript. Catholic University of Louvain, Louvain-la-Neuve, Belgium.

EUROPEAN JOURNAL OF WORK AND ORGANIZATIONAL PSYCHOLOGY, 1999, 8 (1), 33–48

An Evaluative Essay on Current Conceptions of Effective Leadership

Gary Yukl

State University of New York at Albany, USA

Theories of transformational and charismatic leadership provide important insights about the nature of effective leadership, but most of the theories have weaknesses in the conceptualization and measurement of leadership processes. The limitations include use of simplistic two-factor models, omission of relevant behaviours, focus on dyadic processes, assumption of heroic leadership, and overreliance on weak methods. I discuss these weaknesses and present results from a study on leader behaviour dimensions to clarify some of my concerns.

INTRODUCTION

Since the late 1980s, theories of transformational and charismatic leadership have been ascendant in the leadership field (e.g. Bass, 1985; Conger & Kanungo, 1987; House, 1977; Shamir, House, & Arthur, 1993; Tichy & Devanna, 1986). In contrast to the rational processes emphasized in earlier theories, the new theories emphasize emotions and values, which are necessary to understand how a leader can influence followers to make self-sacrifices, commit to ideological objectives, and achieve much more than they initially believed was possible. The new theories also recognize the importance of symbolic behaviour and the role of the leader in making events meaningful for followers. It is evident that the new theories provide important insights about the nature of effective leadership. Nevertheless, proponents of these theories have exaggerated their uniqueness and capacity to explain effective leadership. As a counter-balance to the hype about the new theories, I will present a more critical appraisal. The focus will be more on transformational leadership than on charismatic leadership. My appraisal will take into account several weaknesses in the conceptualization and measurement of leadership processes. I will discuss the omission of relevant leader behaviours, the neglect of group and organizational processes, and over-reliance on weak research methods. I will begin by describing the

Requests for reprints should be addressed to G. Yukl, State University of New York at Albany, 1400 Washington Avenue, Albany, New York 12222, USA; email: G.yukl@albany.edu limitations of two-factor models from a historical perspective that considers earlier theories as well as the newer ones.

LIMITATIONS OF TWO-FACTOR MODELS

A common approach for describing leadership is in terms of a two-factor model. Most of the well-known theories of leadership effectiveness were initially formulated using a two-factor conception of leader behaviour or traits. Examples include task-oriented versus relations-oriented leadership, autocratic versus participative leadership, leadership versus management, transformational versus transactional leadership, and charismatic versus noncharismatic leadership. These dichotomies provide some insights, but they also oversimplify a complex phenomenon and encourage stereotyping of individual leaders. Four of the two-factor models will be examined in more detail to illustrate how we continue to favour simplistic leadership theories.

Task Versus Relations Leadership

From the 1950s through to the 1970s, a prominent way to conceptualize leadership behaviour was in terms of concern for task objectives versus concern for people (or relations). The early Ohio State Leadership Studies (Fleishman, 1953) provided evidence that task and relations behaviour are distinct dimensions, and several subsequent theories incorporated this two-factor conception (e.g. path-goal theory, leader substitutes theory, LPC contingency theory, "high–high" theory). Studies on the implications of the two behaviours for leadership effectiveness have not yielded consistent results (Yukl, 1998). Survey studies using behaviour description questionnaires failed to provide much support for the idea that effective leaders have high scores on both dimensions. A refined version of the "high–high" theory is that effective leaders integrate task and people concerns in a way that is relevant for the situation, rather than merely using task and relations behaviour to the maximum extent (Blake & Mouton, 1982; Sashkin & Fulmer, 1988). This theory has never been adequately tested.

The two-factor conceptualization of leader behaviour is limited as a basis for theory building. In any given situation, some aspects of task-oriented (or relations-oriented) behaviour will be more relevant than other aspects. A theory that uses the broad categories rather than specific component behaviours cannot accurately describe how effective leaders vary their behaviour across situations. Moreover, the task and relations categories (as defined in the questionnaires used to measure them) do not include some types of leadership behaviour that are relevant for understanding effective leadership. Examples include visioning, leading by example, symbolic behaviour, management of meaning, and change-oriented leadership.

Autocratic Versus Participative Leadership

Another popular way to conceptualize leadership during this same period of time was the distinction between autocratic and participative leadership. A large number of studies were conducted to test the proposition that participative leadership is more effective than autocratic leadership. The results were weak and inconsistent (e.g. Cotton, Vollrath, Froggatt, Lengneck-Hall, & Jennings, 1988; Leana, Locke, & Schweiger, 1990), in part because the researchers asked the wrong question. Power sharing is an important aspect of leadership, but classifying leaders in terms of two extreme styles (autocratic vs. participative) fails to accurately portray the complexities of the process. Leaders can select from a wide variety of decision procedures, and most leaders use different procedures for different types of decisions. Effective leaders vary their use of decision procedures and select a procedure that is appropriate for the immediate situation (e.g. Vroom & Jago, 1988; Vroom & Yetton, 1973).

Most of the studies on participative leadership measured only the average amount of participation used by a leader (across subordinates and decisions), and the researchers did not take into account situational contingencies. In their pre-occupation with demonstrating that leaders should be highly participative, most researchers paid little attention to the question of whether the subordinates are prepared, able, and motivated to participate. Leaders have many opportunities to create conditions that will facilitate the success of participation and delegation. These conditions include subordinate clarity and agreement about objectives, skills in problem solving, individual and collective self-efficacy, access to essential information, and cohesiveness and trust among group members. Participative leadership must be combined with other types of leadership behaviour (e.g. supporting, inspiring, coaching, informing, team building, con-flict management, and leading meetings) to be effective, and the appropriate mix of behaviours will depend on the situation.

Leadership Versus Management

Some theorists differentiate between leaders and managers according to their objectives and time orientation (Bennis & Nanus, 1985; Zaleznik, 1977). Leading and managing are seen as two mutually exclusive processes requiring different skills and personality traits. According to these theorists, "leaders" are oriented toward change and long-term effectiveness, whereas "managers" are oriented toward stability and short-term efficiency. People with a managerial profile are assumed to be incapable of inspiring and leading major change in organizations, and people with a leader profile are viewed as unwilling to accept the existing strategy (even when it is appropriate) and work to refine it. Some theorists make an even sharper distinction by describing managers as people who exhibit only negative behaviours such as micromanaging activities, compulsively monitoring and controlling subordinates, and fixating on cost reduction. A more credible view is that people can use a mix of leading and (positive) managing behaviours (Hickman, 1990; Kotter, 1990). A successful executive must be skilled enough to understand the situation and flexible enough to adjust the mix of behaviours as the situation changes.

A key situational variable determining the optimal mix of behaviours is the external environment faced by an organization (Miller & Friesen, 1984; Tushman & Romanelli, 1985). Change-oriented leadership seems more appropriate in times of environmental turmoil when it is necessary to make strategic changes to deal with major threats and opportunities. A "managerial" orientation seems more appropriate when the external environment is relatively stable, the organization is prospering, and it is essential to maintain efficient, reliable operations (e.g. high productivity, high quality, low cost, on-time delivery). Efficiency and adaptation are competing objectives, because actions that enhance one objective may undermine the other. High levels of efficiency can be achieved by actions such as organizing around the strategy, developing a strong supporting culture, refining work processes, establishing norms and standards, and investing in specialized personnel, facilities, or equipment. However, these actions reduce flexibility and make it more difficult to change strategies and work processes in response to new environmental threats and opportunities. Adaptation to a changing environment can be achieved by making major changes in strategy, structure, and work processes. However, these actions tend to reduce short-term efficiency, because they require an investment of extra resources, involve a period of difficult adjustment and relearning, and stimulate disruptive conflict as people seek to protect their power and status. As yet there has been little research to examine what effective leaders do to achieve an appropriate balance between efficiency and adaptation. Stereotyping leaders and managers as opposites detracts attention from empirical research on this important issue.

Transformational Versus Transactional Leadership

Bass (1985) proposed a two-factor model of transformational and transactional leadership based on an earlier distinction made by Burns (1978). Behaviours defining the two types of leadership processes are measured with the Multifactor Leadership Questionnaire (MLQ). The components of transformational and transactional behaviour have varied somewhat across different versions of the questionnaire, and more component behaviours have been added to the recent versions (Bass, 1996; Bass & Avolio, 1990). Transformational leadership includes individualized consideration, intellectual stimulation, idealized influence (charisma), and inspirational motivation. Transactional leadership includes contingent reward behaviour, passive management-by-exception, and active management-by-exception (a form of monitoring). Factor analyses of the

MLQ usually support the proposed distinction between transformational and transactional behaviour, but positive reward behaviour sometimes loads on the transformational factor instead of the transactional factor. In a meta-analytical review of 39 studies, Lowe, Kroeck, and Sivasubramaniam (1996) found that three key elements of transformational leadership correlated positively with subordinate satisfaction and performance. Results for contingent reward behaviour were weaker and less consistent, but it was also correlated positively with the criteria. Management-by-exception was not related to leader effectiveness. Two recently added scales in the MLQ (inspirational motivation and active management-by-exception) were not included in the meta-analysis.

Although no single theory should be expected to include all aspects of leadership behaviour, use of the label "full range leadership theory" by Bass (1996) invites critical evaluation of completeness. Despite the fact that recent versions of the MLQ have expanded the range of behaviours somewhat, the questionnaire still lacks scales on several aspects of leadership behaviour that are relevant for understanding leadership effectiveness. Key omissions include some task behaviours (e.g. clarifying, planning), some relations behaviours (e.g. team building, networking), and some change-oriented behaviours (e.g. scanning and analysis of the external environment, strategy reformulation, political activities to build support for change, reorganization to support a new strategy). Another omission is participative leadership (e.g. consultation, delegation). Bass (1996) proposed that transformational and transactional leadership can be either directive (autocratic) or participative, but the MLQ does not systematically measure this relevant aspect of leader behaviour. Finally, the MLQ does not include some aspects of charismatic leadership (e.g. nontraditional behaviours, impression management, expressive communication). Most researchers who use the MLQ fail to control for the possible effects of unmeasured behaviours that may be confounded with transformational or transactional leadership. When positive correlations are found in survey research, they are automatically attributed to the behaviours that are measured.

The idea that charisma is an essential component of transformational leadership is a questionable assumption based on results from survey research with the MLQ. In contrast to the survey research, descriptive research using observation and interviews to study transformational leadership in managers found that they were not charismatic in the usual sense of the word (e.g. Bennis & Nanus, 1985; Kouzes & Posner, 1987; Tichy & Devanna, 1986). The managers of successful teams and effective organizations were seldom viewed as superhuman by subordinates or peers. With a few exceptions, they were not colourful, larger than life figures who made spellbinding speeches and used nontraditional behaviours to manage impressions. Thus, the meaning of the questionnaire results showing charisma as the core component of transformational leadership is difficult to interpret. The finding that transformational leadership is prevalent among managers at all levels in most types of organizations also raises doubts about what is really being measured. The survey results suggest that many leaders are transformational, yet my experience in studying and training managers fails to support this conclusion. Some managers use some of the behaviours some of the time, but few managers use most of the behaviours whenever they are relevant. How many managers do you know that are really transformational, much less charismatic?

LEVEL OF CONCEPTUALIZATION

Leadership can be conceptualized at different levels (e.g. individual, dyadic, group, organizational). By "level" I mean the identity of the followers and the processes explaining leadership effectiveness, not the leader's level of authority or the type of statistical analysis that is used. In most theories and research on effective leadership there has been a strong bias toward description of leadership processes at the dyadic level, which involves the interaction between a leader and one individual follower. Key questions at this level are how to develop a co-operative, trusting relationship with a follower, and how to influence a follower to be more motivated and committed.

The research on dyadic processes provides important insights about leadership, but it often underestimates the importance of the context in which a dyadic relationship occurs. The group perspective considers not only leader influence on individual members (on their role clarity, skill development, commitment to task objectives, and access to necessary information and resources), but also leader influence on how well the work is organized to utilize personnel and resources, how well group activities are co-ordinated, the amount of member agreement about objectives and priorities, the extent to which members trust each other and co-operate in accomplishing task objectives, the extent of member identification with the group, and confidence in the capacity of the group to attain its objectives. Group processes are largely ignored in most theories of transformational and charismatic leadership, and these theories do not explicitly incorporate leadership behaviours such as organizing, co-ordinating, team building, and facilitating group decisions. One exception is the charismatic leadership theory of Shamir et al. (1993), which recognizes the importance of leader influence on follower identification with the group and perception of collective efficacy.

Theories conceptualized at the group level provide a better understanding of leadership effectiveness than dyadic theories, but they also have some important limitations. Groups usually exist in a larger social system, and to understand effective leadership requires consideration of organizational processes as well as group-level processes (Hunt, 1991). The survival and prosperity of an organization depends on effective adaptation to the environment. Adaptation is improved by anticipating consumer needs and desires, assessing the actions and plans of competitors, evaluating likely constraints and threats (e.g. government regulation, input scarcity, hostile actions by enemies), and identifying marketable products and services that the organization has unique capabilities to provide. An essential leadership function is to help the organization adapt to its environment and acquire resources needed to survive. Some examples of relevant activities include gathering and interpreting information about the environment, identifying core competencies that provide competitive advantage, negotiating agreements that are favourable to the organization, influencing outsiders to have a favourable impression of the organization and its products, gaining co-operation and support from outsiders upon whom the organization is dependent, and recruiting new members. Survival and prosperity also depend on the efficiency of the transformation process used by the organization to produce its products and services. Efficiency is increased by finding more rational ways to differentiate subunits, and by deciding how to make the best use of available technology, resources, and personnel. Some examples of leadership responsibilities include designing an appropriate organization structure, determining authority relationships, and co-ordinating operations across specialized subunits of the organization.

Leadership processes at the organization level are given little attention in the transformational leadership theory formulated by Bass (1985). Some of the transformational leadership theories based on descriptive research (e.g. Bennis & Nanus, 1985; Kouzes & Posner, 1987; Tichy & Devanna, 1986) acknowledge leader contributions to organizational level processes, but they only begin to describe how these leadership processes occur. Some theories of charismatic leadership describe organizational level processes, but only in relation to selected topics (e.g. leadership succession, institutionalization of charisma). Research on how leaders influence organization culture and implement major changes has increased over the past decade, but more such research is needed. Theories of transformational and charismatic leadership should incorporate more of the relevant concepts and findings from the strategic leadership literature (see Finkelstein & Hambrick, 1996).

BIASED CONCEPTIONS OF LEADERSHIP PROCESSES

Most transformational leadership theories reflect the implicit assumptions associated with the "heroic leadership" stereotype. One assumption is that an effective leader will influence followers to make self-sacrifices and exert exceptional effort. This orientation steers research in the direction of identifying the essential traits, skills, and behaviours of individual leaders for motivating subordinates, rather than toward understanding reciprocal influence processes in dyads and groups. Even though the importance of empowerment is acknowledged in transformational leadership, researchers study how leaders use power and influence to overcome resistance, not how resistance can be a source of energy that enables people to collectively make better decisions about what type of change is needed. Inspirational motivation includes encouraging subordinates to embrace, disseminate, and implement the vision, but not encouraging subordinates to challenge the vision or develop a better one. Intellectual stimulation includes communicating novel ideas to a subordinate, but not providing opportunities for subordinates to learn from experience and helping them interpret experience in a meaningful way.

Charismatic leadership theories reflect an even stronger bias toward heroic leadership. Researchers with this bias seek to identify attributes that increase leader influence over subordinates, not to describe how the same qualities can be both a strength and weakness for a leader. For example, expressing strong convictions, acting confident, and taking decisive action can create an impression of exceptional expertise, but it can also discourage relevant feedback from followers. Articulating nontraditional ideas in an emotional way and displaying unconventional behaviour can help the leader win loyal followers, but these charismatic behaviours can also create some dedicated opponents who strive to undermine the leader and his or her programmes.

In contrast to the heroic leader, a very different conception of leadership is in terms of influence processes that contribute to the collective and individual capacity of people to accomplish their work roles effectively. Instead of focusing on a single person who (as the designated leader) influences followers, many people are viewed as contributors to the overall process of leadership in organizations. This conception of shared leadership does not require an individual who is exceptional or who can perform all of the essential leadership functions, only a set of people who collectively perform them. Different people may perform a particular leadership function at different times, and different functions may be performed by different people (e.g. whomever is most qualified). This conception also recognizes that most people have dual roles as a leader and follower in the same organization. The leadership actions of any individual are much less important than the collective leadership provided by many members of the organization. This perspective encourages researchers to examine the compatibility, consistency, diffusion, and relevance of leadership processes in relation to the situation as determinants of organizational effectiveness. Shared leadership is especially relevant for the increasing number of organizations using self-managed teams, executive teams, flexible structures, partnering, and joint ventures. Unfortunately, few researchers seem interested in studying shared leadership processes in groups and organizations.

A STUDY ON LEADERSHIP BEHAVIOUR DIMENSIONS

In 1996, I conducted an exploratory field study to see how well the popular two-factor conceptions of leadership hold up when items representing all of them are included in the same questionnaire (Yukl, 1997). The sample for the survey included 318 direct reports of 48 managers in several US companies and government agencies. Respondents described the leadership behaviour of their immediate boss. It was not feasible to administer several complete questionnaires to the respondents (the short versions of the MLQ and the MPS were not available at the time), but the questionnaire developed for my study included some representative items from several widely used instruments. The questionnaire covered a wide range of behaviours and included items describing leadership behaviours relevant for group and organizational processes as well as dyadic processes.

The results showed that none of the two-factor models discussed earlier explained an adequate amount of the variance. A three-factor model worked better, but it only accounted for only 55% of the item variance. Table 1 shows representative items with their factor loadings. Task-oriented behaviour (the T-factor) included operational planning, clarifying task roles, and monitoring operations and performance quality. Relations-oriented behaviour (the R-factor) included being supportive and considerate, providing recognition, providing coaching and mentoring, encouraging participation in decision making, and encouraging co-operation. Change-oriented behaviour (the C-factor) included identifying external threats and opportunities, envisioning new possibilities, proposing nontraditional strategies, and influencing political support for change.

The questionnaire included some items on key aspects of consideration and initiating structure, as defined in the LBDQ and instruments derived from it. As expected, the consideration items loaded on the R-factor and the initiating structure items loaded on the T-factor. However, it was obvious that the R-factor is much broader than consideration and the T-factor is much broader than initiating structure. The primary component of LBDQ consideration is supportive leadership behaviour, whereas the R-factor also includes behaviours such as recognizing, consulting, and developing. The primary component of LBDQ initiating structure is clarifying of subordinate roles, whereas the T-factor also includes goal setting, monitoring and operational planning. The additional items for the T and R factors came primarily from the MPS. The T and R dimensions can be viewed as a refinement of the two-factor taxonomy identified by the Ohio State leadership studies, whereas the C dimension is an extension of that research into a new behaviour domain.

The questionnaire used in my study also included items from most of the scales in the Managerial Practices Survey (MPS; Kim & Yukl, 1996; Yukl, Wall, & Lepsinger, 1990). The MPS is representative of several leadership questionnaires that measure a variety of specific behaviours or skills. These questionnaires have been widely used for many years to provide feedback to managers, but they are seldom used for leadership research. In the factor analysis, items from three MPS scales (clarifying, planning/organizing, internal monitoring) loaded on the T-factor. Items from five MPS scales loaded on the R-factor (supporting, consulting, delegating, recognizing, and developing). The results for consultation and delegation suggest that participative leadership is

TABLE 1
Factor Loadings for Representative Items

Behaviour Item and Primary Category	T	R	C
Task-oriented behaviour:			
14. Plans in detail how to accomplish an important task or project.	0.74		
1. Provides a clear explanation of your responsibilities with regard to a task or project.	0.72		
12. Clearly explains what results are expected for a task or project.	0.69		
54. Determines what resources are needed to carry out a project.	0.65		
4. Determines how to organize and co-ordinate work activities to avoid delays, duplication of effort, and wasted resources.	0.62		
34. Checks work progress against plans to see if it is on target.	0.62		
Relations-oriented behaviour:			
20. Provides encouragement and support when you have a difficult or stressful task.		0.78	
72. Backs you up and supports you in a difficult situation.		0.70	
42. Gives you credit for helpful ideas and suggestions		0.69	
6. Consults with you to get your reactions and suggestions before making a decision that affects you.		0.66	
22. Provides opportunities to develop your skills and show what you can do.		0.65	
9. Expresses confidence in your ability to carry out a difficult task.		0.64	
Change-oriented behaviour:			
28. Proposes new and creative ideas for improving products, services, or processes.			0.67
52. Is confident and optimistic when proposing a major change.			0.67
43. Takes a long-term perspective on problems and opportunities facing the organization.			0.64
3. Describes a clear, appealing vision of what the organization can accomplish or become.			0.57
35. Negotiates persuasively with people outside the work unit to get agreements or approvals necessary to implement a major change.			0.53
32. Studies the products and activities of competitors to get ideas for improving things in his/her organizational unit.			0.53

Note: Some items were shortened; factor loadings less than .30 are not shown.

primarily a relations-oriented behaviour. Elements of three other MPS scales (informing, rewarding, and team building/conflict management) also loaded on the R-factor. Some items from three MPS scales (problem solving, inspiring/motivating, external networking) loaded on the C-factor. The very limited coverage of change-oriented behaviours in the MPS is the likely reason it does not yield a separate factor for change-oriented leadership.

The results are also relevant for evaluating the leader versus manager dichotomy. The study provides positive examples of efficiency-oriented versus change-oriented behaviour to replace the polarized stereotypes (i.e. bureaucratic manager versus inspirational leader) advocated by some theorists. There was no support for the idea that most executives use only one type of behaviour almost exclusively, or that they can be grouped into distinct manager or leader "types" based on their pattern of scores. Most managers appeared to use a mix of the different behaviours. Unfortunately, it was not possible to determine if the behaviour pattern for a manager was related to the environment of the organization or to independent criteria of leadership effectiveness. These questions need to be explored in subsequent research with a more intensive methodology.

The questionnaire in this study also included items adapted from key scales in the MLQ. The factor loadings for these items are shown in Table 2. The items on individualized consideration had primary loadings on the R-factor, although some of them also had secondary loadings on another factor. The items on other aspects of transformational leadership usually loaded on the R-factor or the C-factor. Items on contingent rewarding (a transactional behaviour) loaded on the R-factor. Active monitoring (a transactional behaviour) loaded on the T-factor. The weak representation of items on change-oriented behaviour in the MLQ may explain why factor analyses of it do not yield a separate C-factor. The weak representation of effective task-oriented behaviours and the strong representation of ineffective task-oriented behaviours (e.g. management-by-exception, *laissez-faire* management) may explain why factor analyses of the MLQ yield a factor for transactional leadership but not for task-oriented behaviour.

A limitation of my study is that it only included sample items from other questionnaires and they were sometimes modified. The research needs to be replicated with the complete version of these instruments and a larger sample. Nevertheless, the results suggest answers to some bothersome questions about the meaning and scope of transformational leadership. As operationally defined in the MLQ, transformational leadership seems to be primarily concerned about motivating subordinates and satisfying their individual needs for attention and personal development. These behaviours are more representative of relations-oriented behaviour than change-oriented behaviour. The motivating behaviours in transformational leadership (e.g. role modeling, visioning) can be used to build commitment to objectives and strategies that are either traditional or revolutionary. In other words, the transformational leadership scale describes a leader who attempts to support and inspire subordinates, but not necessarily to make major changes in the objectives, strategies, or structures of the organizational unit. As operationally defined in the MLQ, transactional leadership seems to be primarily concerned about manipulating and controlling subordinates. Transactional leadership has a negative connotation, much like the "managing" stereotype in the leader/manager dichotomy described earlier. Most of the positive task-oriented functions that are a necessary part of effective leadership are not included in the scale or the theory.

TABLE 2
Factor Loadings for Items on Transformational or Transactional Leadership

Behaviour Item	T	R	C
Transformational leadership:			
49. Treats each subordinate as an individual with different needs, abilities, and aspirations.		0.61	0.35
40. Talks about the importance of mutual trust among members.		0.62	0.34
63. Behaves in a way that is consistent with the ideals and values he/she espouses.		0.57	
16. Provides advice and coaching to help you develop new skills.	0.31	0.56	
45. Encourages you to look a problem from different perspectives.	0.31	0.49	
24. Describes exciting new opportunities for the organization.		0.34	0.59
33. Talks with conviction about his/her values and ideals.		0.33	0.49
39. Makes personal sacrifices and goes beyond selfinterest for the benefit of the organization.		0.36	0.41
11. Questions traditional assumptions and beliefs about the best way to do things.			0.40
Transactional leadership:			
70. Rewards subordinates for effective performance and contributions to the organization.		0.64	
31. Explains what must be done to get rewards such as a pay increase or promotion.		0.47	0.30
54. Checks on the quality of your work.	0.56		
58. Asks you to report on your progress.	0.58		

Note: Factor loadings less than 0.30 are not shown.

LIMITATIONS OF RESEARCH METHODS

Static correlational analysis of data from survey questionnaires continues to be the dominant method for research on transformational and charismatic leadership in large organizations. Critics of traditional quantitative research contend that it has an inherent bias toward exaggerating the importance of individual leaders. Most leadership questionnaires ask subordinates or peers to rate retrospectively how often or how much a leader exhibited some behaviour over a period of several months or years. This frequency format may reduce the relevance of the measures, especially if a scale has many behaviours that are ineffective when overused or used at inappropriate times (Shipper, 1991). Frequency ratings on individual behaviours are poorly suited for studying leadership as a dynamic process embedded in complex social systems. How often a particular category of behaviour is used is less important than whether it is used in a skilful manner at an appropriate time in the sequence of events. Moreover, the effectiveness of any individual behaviour depends in part on the overall pattern of leadership behaviour.

Some of the critics of questionnaire-correlational research advocate greater use of descriptive methods such as observation, interviews, and intensive case studies (e.g. Bryman, Bresnen, Beardworth, & Keil, 1988). These methods appear better suited for studying leadership from a systems perspective at the group or organizational level. However, the descriptive research methods also have limitations, regardless of whether the form of data analysis is qualitative or quantitative (e.g. Martinko & Gardner, 1985). The limitations of each type of methodology make it desirable to use multiple methods whenever feasible (Jick, 1979; Yukl & Van Fleet, 1982). Unfortunately, most researchers select a single method that is traditional and easy to use. Few researchers conduct longitudinal studies or use multiple methods (which may produce inconsistent results that are difficult to explain).

Faster progress in our understanding of transformational and charismatic leadership will require use of more varied research methods and increased reliance on intensive, longitudinal studies. In one example of a novel approach (House, Spangler, & Woycke, 1991), researchers analysed the content of speeches of US Presidents and biographies by their cabinet members to identify leader behaviours and traits that differentiated between charismatic and non-charismatic leaders and correlated with indicators of leadership effectiveness. In another example (Roberts, 1985; Roberts & Bradley, 1988), researchers conducted an intensive, longitudinal case study of a woman who held two successive positions as an educational administrator (one in which she was regarded as charismatic and one in which she was not) to identify the behaviours, processes, conditions, and outcomes associated with attributions of charisma.

Leadership researchers are not limited to a choice between survey studies and descriptive field studies. Controlled experiments in a laboratory setting (e.g. Howell & Frost, 1989; Kirkpatrick & Locke, 1996) or a field setting (e.g. Barling, Weber, & Kelloway, 1996) are effective research methods that should be utilized more often. Whenever possible, field experiments (or quasi-experiments) should be conducted over a fairly long time interval with a combination of descriptive methods (e.g. interviews, observation, diaries) and repeated application of questionnaires. Realistic simulations also have promise for studying particular aspects of leadership, especially when the simulations are conducted over repeated sessions with actual managers (not undergraduates). Finally, the benefits of diverse research methods can be realized by use of comparative case studies that include quantitative measures (which are feasible when there are enough cases) as well as detailed ethnographic description.

CONCLUSIONS

Theories of transformational and charismatic leadership contribute to our understanding of leadership effectiveness, but their uniqueness and contribution have been exaggerated. In much of the hype about the newer theories, there is a tendency to ignore or discount earlier theory and research on leadership behaviour. Some transformational behaviours (e.g. individualized consideration, active monitoring) are already represented in earlier theory and research; others (e.g. intellectual stimulation, idealized influence) are vague about what a leader really does. A similar criticism can be made for charismatic leadership theory. More attention should be devoted to clearly identifying the behaviours relevant for transformational and charismatic leadership.

Some theory refinement is desirable to correct the deficiencies discussed earlier. The description of dyadic processes should be supplemented with a description of leadership processes in groups and organizations. The inherent assumption of heroic leadership should be replaced by a broader conception of leadership as a shared, reciprocal influence process. The scope of the core behaviours should be expanded to include other types of leadership behaviour known to be relevant. The practical implications of the theories for organizations need to be identified more carefully. Transformational leadership may be widely relevant for all types of organizations, as claimed by its proponents, but the relevance of charismatic leadership appears to be overstated. A charismatic leader is not always necessary, and strong charismatics pose many potential dangers for organizations. More research is needed to determine if it is possible to have the potential benefits of charismatic leadership without the negative consequences.

On a different note, some critics have expressed concern about the ethics of influencing followers to be constantly doing more for the organization (Stephens, D'Intino, & Victor, 1995). It is not always in the best interests of employees to maximize benefits for other stakeholders (such as owners or customers). Much of the current interest in "ethical leadership" and "servant leadership" seems to reflect the issue of how a leader's actions affect different parties (who gains and in what ways?). Theories of effective leadership should deal more directly with the question of how to balance the competing values inherent in organizations. Researchers studying leadership should use criteria of leadership effectiveness that take these complexities into account.

The promise of the new theories will not be realized until the research on them improves. Despite all the hype about a "new paradigm" for studying leadership, most of the research uses the same superficial methods that have been prevalent for decades. Correlating one popular questionnaire with another, or conducting endless replications of criterion-related correlations tells us little about effective leadership. A different approach is needed to gain a deeper understanding of effective leadership in organizations. We need to use methods that are powerful and appropriate for the research question, rather than relying so much on methods that are easy and samples that are convenient. A greater variety of research methods should be used, and the mix of methods should include more intensive, longitudinal studies that examine leadership from a systems perspective.

In summary, my overall assessment of transformational and charismatic leadership theories is that they make an important contribution to the literature, but they should not be heralded as a revolutionary approach that makes all the earlier theories obsolete. I do not mean to diminish the very real contribution made by these theories, but only to put them into proper perspective and suggest ways to make them more useful.

REFERENCES

Barling, J., Weber, T., & Kelloway, E.K. (1996). Effects of transformational leadership training on attitudinal and financial outcomes: A field experiment. *Journal of Applied Psychology, 81*, 827–832.

Bass, B.M. (1985). *Leadership and performance beyond expectations*. New York: Free Press.

Bass, B.M. (1996). *A new paradigm of leadership: An inquiry into transformational leadership*. Alexandria, VA: US Army Research Institute for the Behavioural and Social Sciences.

Bass, B.M., & Avolio, B.J. (1990). *Multifactor leadership questionnaire*. Palo Alto, CA: Consulting Psychologists Press.

Bennis, W.G., & Nanus, B. (1985). *Leaders: The strategies for taking charge*. New York: Harper & Row.

Blake, R.R., & Mouton, J.S. (1982). Management by grid principles or situationalism: Which? *Group and Organization Studies, 7*, 207–210.

Bryman, A., Bresnen, M., Beardworth, A., & Keil, T. (1988). Qualitative research and the study of leadership. *Human Relations, 41*, 13–30.

Burns, J.M. (1978). *Leadership*. New York: Harper & Row.

Conger, J.A., & Kanungo, R. (1987). Toward a behavioural theory of charismatic leadership in organizational settings. *Academy of Management Review, 12*, 637–647.

Cotton, J.L., Vollrath, D.A., Froggatt, K.L., Lengneck-Hall, M.L., & Jennings, K.R. (1988). Employee participation: Diverse forms and different outcomes. *Academy of Management Review, 13*, 8–22.

Finkelstein, S., & Hambrick, D.C. (1996). *Strategic leadership: Top executives and their effects on organizations*. Minneapolis/St Paul, MN: West.

Fleishman, E.A. (1953). The description of supervisory behaviour. *Personnel Psychology, 37*, 1–6.

Hickman, C.F. (1990). *Mind of a manager, soul of a leader*. New York: Wiley.

House, R.J. (1977). A 1976 theory of charismatic leadership. In J.G. Hunt & L.L. Larson (Eds.), *Leadership: The cutting edge*. Carbondale, IL: Southern Illinois University Press.

House, R.J., Spangler, W.D., & Woycke, J. (1991). Personality and charisma in the US presidency: A psychological theory of leadership effectiveness. *Administrative Science Quarterly, 36*, 364-396.

Howell, J.M., & Frost, P. (1989). A laboratory study of charismatic leadership. *Organizational Behaviour and Human Decision Processes, 43*, 243–269.

Hunt, J.G. (1991). *Leadership: A new synthesis*. Newbury Park, CA: Sage.

Jick, T.D. (1979). Mixing qualitative and quantitative methods: Triangulation in action. *Administrative Science Quarterly, 24*, 602–611.

Kim, H., & Yukl, G. (1996). Relationships of managerial effectiveness and advancement to self-reported and subordinate-reported leadership behaviours from the multiple-linkage model. *Leadership Quarterly, 6*, 361–377.

Kirkpatrick, S.A., & Locke, E.A. (1996). Direct and indirect effects of three core charismatic leadership components on performance and attitudes. *Journal of Applied Psychology, 81*, 36–51.

Kotter, J.P. (1990). *A force for change: How leadership differs from management*. New York: Free Press.

Kouzes, J.M., & Posner, B.Z. (1987). *The leadership challenge*. San Francisco: Jossey-Bass.

Leana, C.R., Locke, E.A., & Schweiger, D.M. (1990). Fact and fiction in analyzing research on participative decision making: A critique of Cotton, Vollrath, Froggatt, Lengnick-Hall, and Jennings. *Academy of Management Review, 15*, 137–146.

Lowe, K.B., Kroeck, K.G., & Sivasubramaniam, N. (1996). Effectiveness correlates of transformational and transactional leadership: A meta-analytic review of the MLQ literature. *Leadership Quarterly, 7*, 385–425.

Martinko, M.J., & Gardner, W.L. (1985). Beyond structured observation: Methodological issues and new directions. *Academy of Management Review, 10*, 676–695.

Miller, D., & Friesen, P.H. (1984). *Organizations: A quantum view.* Englewood Cliffs, NJ: Prentice-Hall.

Roberts, N.C. (1985). Transforming leadership: A process of collective action. *Human Relations, 38*, 1023–1046.

Roberts, N.C., & Bradley, R.T. (1988). Limits of charisma. In J.A. Conger & R.N. Kanungo (Eds.), *Charismatic leadership: The elusive factor in organizational effectiveness* (pp. 253–275). San Francisco: Jossey-Bass.

Sashkin, M., & Fulmer, R.M. (1988). Toward an organizational leadership theory. In J.G. Hunt, B.R. Baliga, H.P. Dachler, & C.A. Schriesheim (Eds.), *Emerging leadership vistas* (pp. 51–65). Lexington, MA: Heath.

Shamir, B., House, R.J., & Arthur, M.B. (1993). The motivational effects of charismatic leadership: A self-concept based theory. *Organization Science, 4*, 1–17.

Shipper, F. (1991). Mastery and frequency of managerial behaviours relative to subunit effectiveness. *Human Relations, 44*, 371–388.

Stephens, C.U., D'Intino, R.S., & Victor, B. (1995). The moral quandary of transformational leadership: Change for whom? In R. Woodman & W. Pasmore (Eds.), *Research in organizational change and development, Vol. 8* (pp. 123–143). Greenwich, CT: JAI Press.

Tichy, N.M., & Devanna, M.A. (1986). *The transformational leader.* New York: John Wiley.

Tushman, M.L., & Romanelli, E. (1985). Organizational evolution: A metamorphosis model of convergence and reorientation. In L.L. Cummings & B.M. Staw (Eds.), *Research in organizational behaviour, Vol. 7* (pp. 171–222). Greenwich, CT: JAI Press.

Vroom, V.H., & Jago, A.G. (1988). *The new leadership: Managing participation in organizations.* Englewood Cliffs, NJ: Prentice-Hall.

Vroom, V.H., & Yetton, P.W. (1973). *Leadership and decision making.* Pittsburgh, PA: University of Pittsburgh Press.

Yukl, G. (1997). *Effective leadership behaviour: A new taxonomy and model.* Paper presented at the Eastern Academy of Management International Conference, Dublin, Ireland.

Yukl, G. (1998). *Leadership in organizations* (4th ed.). Englewood Cliffs, NJ: Prentice-Hall.

Yukl, G.A., & Van Fleet, D. (1982). Cross-situational, multi-method research on military leader effectiveness. *Organizational Behaviour and Human Performance, 30*, 87–108.

Yukl, G., Wall, S., & Lepsinger, R. (1990). Preliminary report on validation of the managerial practices survey. In K.E. Clark & M.B. Clark (Eds.), *Measures of leadership* (pp. 223–238). West Orange, NJ: Leadership Library of America.

Zaleznik, A. (1977). Leaders and managers: Are they different? *Harvard Business Review*, May–June, 67–78.

EUROPEAN JOURNAL OF WORK AND ORGANIZATIONAL PSYCHOLOGY, 1999, 8 (1), 49–71

Leadership in Boundaryless Organizations: Disposable or Indispensable?

Boas Shamir

Department of Sociology and Anthropology, The Hebrew University, Jerusalem, Israel

The emergence of "post-bureaucratic" "boundaryless" organizations raises questions about the role of leadership in such organizational forms. In this article I analyse the basic characteristics of emerging organizational forms and offer a theory-guided speculation about the function and nature of leadership within such forms. The analysis exposes a basic dilemma: On the one hand, the temporary, ad-hoc and "virtual" nature of new organizational arrangements, in combination with greater tendencies toward equality and participation, seem to reduce the need and scope for traditional leadership in organizations. On the other hand, the weakening of both bureaucratic and cultural mechanisms of control and co-ordination seems to increase the need and scope for strong leadership. A related dilemma concerns the need for leaders to serve simultaneously as both agents of change and "centres of gravity" in organizations that cope with rapidly changing environments. These dilemmas pose practical challenges for leaders and theoretical challenges for leadership scholars. I discuss the appropriateness of current leadership theories to meet these challenges and offer directions for further theoretical developments.

INTRODUCTION

The social-scientific history of the concept of leadership, like that of other concepts in the social sciences, can be characterized by a cyclical or pendulum-like movement, between alternating periods of enthusiasm and disillusionment. The 1970s was a period of relative disillusionment, as illustrated by a suggestion to abandon the concept (Miner, 1975), and by the title of a famous collection of essays from that period: "Leadership: Where else can we go?" (McCall & Lombardo, 1978). The 1980s and 1990s, in contrast, have been a period of relative enthusiasm around the study of leadership, as reflected in the dominance

Requests for reprints should be addressed to B. Shamir, Dept. of Sociology and Anthropology, The Hebrew University, Jerusalem 91905, Israel; email: msshamir@pluto.mscc.huji.ac.il

The author wishes to thank the following individuals and groups for their comments on an earlier draft of this paper: Michael B. Arthur, Bruce J. Avolio, Amalya Oliver, participants in the WORC workshop on transformational/charismatic leadership, Tilburg University, 3–5 May, 1997, and participants in sub–theme 9 of the 13th EGOS Colloquium, Budapest, 3–5 July 1997.

of transformational and charismatic leadership theories. These theories present, analyse, and often even advocate "strong leadership" which is assumed or hypothesized to have profound impact on people and organizations (Bass, 1985; Bryman, 1992; Conger & Kanungo, 1988; House & Shamir, 1993).

As we approach the end of the 1990s the swinging back of the pendulum may be expected, and indeed may already be felt. Several trends, such as the increasing prominence of team concepts in the field of management, the increasing prevalence of computer-mediated technologies and the development of more flexible and "boundaryless" organizational forms, create the conditions for the rejection of the "strong leadership" theories of the 1980s and 1990s and the adoption of "weak leadership" theories instead. Weak leadership theories, appearing under names such as "self-leadership", "shared leadership", and "substitutes for leadership", are attractive due to their implication of reduced power distance and greater equality among organizational members. Such theories may also seem to be more suitable for flattened and transient systems that employ remote, virtually connected, and temporary members.

In this article, I examine the suitability of the currently dominant paradigm of "neo-charismatic" leadership theories to the changing organizational forms. After characterizing the emerging model of the boundaryless and flexible organization, I briefly examine possible scenarios in which leaders become "disposable", and leadership is seen as becoming less critical to the functioning of organizations. Further analysis of the central features of the emerging new organizational models leads me, however, to an opposite scenario. In this scenario, leadership, far from becoming disposable, is becoming indispensable because it has to compensate for the weakening of traditional integration and coordination mechanisms. I conclude from this analysis that the strong leadership portrayed by the transformational and "neo-charismatic" theories of the 1980s and 1990s may be even more appropriate for post-industrial, post-bureaucratic, and post-modern organizations than it has ever been for the bureaucratic organizations of the industrial era.

I submit, however, that since the main functions of leadership in boundaryless organizations are likely to be integrative, more scholarly attention should be given to the question of how can leaders perform the integrative role under conditions characterized by transience and remoteness of membership and rapid environmental change. More attention should be given to the increasing complexity of the role of leaders and the fact that they increasingly have to balance contradictory tendencies: to serve as guardians of continuity and stability, and at the same time to serve as champions and facilitators of change. The new conditions and role requirements present leaders with major practical challenges, and leadership scholars with major theoretical challenges. The original concept of charisma, for instance, was suitable to explain infrequent periods of change, but is no longer appropriate in a world characterized by constant change. I conclude by examining the concept of identity as a possible anchor for theoretical efforts that try to explain how leaders can perform the seemingly contradictory demands of serving as both agents of change and "centres of gravity" at the same time.

CLARIFICATION OF TERMS

Before embarking on my theoretical speculation I should clarify what I mean by the term "leadership" in this article, and what I mean by "strong" and "weak" leadership. Traditional concepts of leadership have come under attack for being too "leader-centred" and equating leadership with the traits and behaviours of the leader. Some writers (e.g. Gemmil & Oakley, 1992; Meindl, 1990; Meindl, Ehrlich, & Dukerich, 1985) have gone as far as claiming that leadership is just an attribution, a romanticization, a social contagion process or a myth which is totally unrelated to the traits or actions of the leaders. Others (e.g. Barker, 1997; Burns, 1978) have adopted a less extreme view and argued that leaders and followers (or members or collaborators) engage in a mutual or reciprocal influence process which changes both leaders and followers.

To some extent I agree with both claims. There is considerable evidence that followers' attribution, projection, transference, romanticization, and other perceptual and social construction processes often contribute to the emergence of leaders and the elevation of their status. Furthermore, leadership is indeed a mutual and reciprocal process, which means, first, that the outcomes of the process are determined by much more than the characteristics, abilities, and behaviours of leaders, and, second, that the leaders themselves are often changed in the process.

I submit, however, that mutual and reciprocal influence processes do not necessarily imply symmetric processes. I further submit, that the term "leadership" is useful only in instances characterized by asymmetrical influence processes, when an individual or a small number of individuals exert disproportionate influence on a larger collectivity. This is not a romantic or "leader-centred" view of leadership in the sense of exaggerating the role of leaders. Leadership is not always necessary or important, and collective action may not always require leadership. However, leaderless collective action should be distinguished from leadership and called by different names. To talk about leadership in the absence of leaders extends the coverage of the term beyond usefulness for practical or social-scientific discourse. I shall therefore reserve the term leadership to processes of disproportionate social influence in which the party that exerts greater influence on others (the leader) can be identified.

According to this definition, there can be no leadership without leaders. Given this definition, for the purposes of this article the terms "strong" and "weak" leadership refer to the extent of influence a salient individual (a leader) or a small group of individuals (a leadership group) exert on their social environment. It should be emphasized that these terms do not refer to the personality characteristics of the leaders, their leadership style, or to the specific nature of their influence. Thus, by strong leadership I do not mean authoritarian leadership, nor do I mean a leadership that creates high levels of obedience or dependency on the part of followers. Strong leadership may be evident, for instance, in the extent of its influence on the empowerment and development of followers. Indeed, it is these aspects of influence that are emphasized by current transformational (Bass, 1985), and "neo-charismatic" (Conger & Kanungo, 1988; Shamir, House, & Arthur, 1993) leadership theories.

THE EMERGING TREND: TOWARDS THE BOUNDARYLESS ORGANIZATION

Scholarly and popular scenarios of organizational futures seem to converge. The literature seems to agree that the faster pace of environmental and technological change, combined with the trend toward globalization and the opportunities created by information and computer-mediated technologies require, and indeed already produce more flexible organizations. One important characteristic of the new form of organization is the obliteration of boundaries within the organization and between the organization and elements in its external environment. This "boundaryless organization" (Davis, 1995; Hirschhorn & Gilmore, 1992) is portrayed as containing less fixed structures and more temporary systems, whose elements, both people and technologies, are assembled and disassembled according to the shifting needs of specific projects. "Organizational action in the new model needs to be viewed in terms of clusters of activity sets whose membership, composition, ownership, and goals are constantly changing, and in which projects rather than positions are central" (Kanter, Stein, & Jick, 1991, p. 13). Both internal and external relationships change, and people move more frequently between firms and industries and within firms. Furthermore, many of them are connected to the organization not only temporarily but also virtually, through networks of computers and terminals.

In current views of the organization the focus shifts from lines and boxes to connections (Mohrman & Cohen, 1995). Such views de-emphasize the organization as a body, a structure, a legal entity, or a collection of people, and emphasize instead the process of organizing (Arthur & Rousseau, 1996). In this literature, the most frequently mentioned organizational arrangements are informal division of labour, information networks, adhocracies, flat structures, decentralization, professional autonomy, loose-coupling, teamwork, and self-regulation (Cascio, 1995). The term "post-bureaucratic" has also been applied to characterize the new organizational forms (Hecksher & Donnellon, 1994).

March (1995, p. 434) summarized these trends in the following manner:

> Throw-away personnel policies, where emphasis is placed on selection and turnover rather than on training and learning have become common in modern

business, politics and marriage. In such a throw-away world, organizations lose important elements of permanence. For various legal and other institutional reasons, they may preserve a semblance of continuity—a corporate name and a skeleton, for example. But they become notably more temporary, as reflected in the ad-hoc construction of project groups or collaborations linked together by constantly changing non-hierarchical networks. These cobweb-like "virtual" organizations are not yet a dominant component of current organizational life, but they appear to be becoming more important.

This trend of change from the bureaucratic organization towards the "boundaryless organization" must have important implications for the practice and study of leadership, but these implications have not yet been discussed by leadership scholars. A possible exception is House (1995, p. 411), who in a recent speculative essay about leadership in the 21st century observed that:

> Scholars and practitioners of management generally concur that organizational leaders in the twenty first century will face a number of important changes that will impose substantial new role demands. These changes include greater demographic diversity of workforces, a faster pace of environmental and technological change, more frequent geopolitical shifts affecting borders and distribution of power among nation states, and increased international competition. The popular and business press expect these changes to result in new and different relationships between employers and employees, organizations and resource suppliers, government and business, and buyers and sellers. If this is the case, business, government and military organizations will need to adopt new strategic approaches and organizational forms. These changes will place new demands on the leaders of tomorrow.

WEAK LEADERSHIP SCENARIOS

Disposable Leaders

Despite some acknowledgment of the potential importance of emerging changes in organizational environments and organizational forms for the theory and practice of organizational leadership, the full implications of these changes have not been spelled out yet. One possible scenario that seems to be implied by some of the futuristic organizational literature is that of the "disposable leaders". This scenario extends the logic of the transience of organizational systems to the phenomenon of leadership. According to this scenario, as organizations increasingly rely on temporary ad hoc arrangements, leadership itself will become such an arrangement, and will therefore be limited both in scope and in duration.

The type of leadership implied by this view is primarily knowledge-based. A person will normally serve as a leader of a group for the duration of a specific project due to a specific knowledge advantage he or she has with regard to that particular project. In such a scenario, the leadership function will shift to another person when the project or the composition of the group changes. Leadership may even shift from one person to another within the framework of the same project, for instance, when a new phase requires a different knowledge base or different network connections. Moreover, since people are expected to have multiple and dynamic roles both within organizations and in different organizations, a person may simultaneously be a leader in one group, and a team member in another. Mohrman and Cohen (1995) have referred to such roles as "quasi-managers".

Collective Leadership

A similar scenario is implied by those who discuss or promote ideas of "shared leadership", "collective leadership", "distributed leadership", or "peer leadership". There may be differences among these ideas in their particulars, but the common element in all of them is that leadership is not concentrated in the hands of a single person or a small group, but is divided and performed by many if not all team members, simultaneously or sequentially (House & Adytia, 1997). For instance, Burns (1996) recently talks about "collective webs of leadership". The idea is not fully developed, but in such webs top-down processes are less important than in traditional leadership models. Leaders, or "initiators" as Burns refers to them, do not only "push" ideas onto members of a collectivity. Members also "pull" ideas from the leader and all the other actors. "To be sure, that initiator must speak some word or take some action that will reach the motivational bases of others, but once that happens, mutual motivation—including self-motivation—is the powerhouse of change, in collectively mobilized collaboration and opposition" (Burns, 1996, p. 25). According to Avolio, Jung, Murry, and Sivasubramaniam (1996) as teams reach higher stages of development they exhibit a greater tendency to share leadership responsibilities. The currently popular terms of "self-directed" or "self-managed" teams imply the transfer of leadership responsibilities from a designated leader to the entire team (e.g. Barker, 1993; Manz & Sims, 1993).

Teleleadership

The disposable leadership and collective leadership scenarios imply a weakening of the traditional leadership role. Such weakening may also be implied by scenarios that depict future organizations as virtual networks (Davidow & Malone, 1992). The term "teleleadership" has been coined by Shamir and Ben-Ari (1999) to refer to the role of the military commander as portrayed in some descriptions of military leadership in the future. They expand (p. 17):

For instance, in the US Army literature about Force XXI ("The Army of Tomorrow") the military commander is portrayed as standing in the middle of an information center and being involved mainly in reading and interpreting information conveyed by electronic means, and transmitting orders and instructions through these same means. Even in field units, the commander is represented less as a leader than as a technological manager or information engineer who stays in the control room or control vehicle, and is therefore physically and socially distant from the majority of his or her subordinates. In line with the growing popularity of such terms as "telework", "telemaintenance", and "telemedicine" we may witness the rise of "teleleadership", a form of distant or synthetic leadership which has no eye-contact with followers, no way of inspiring confidence by non-verbal cues, and very limited possibilities for displaying physical courage or for leading through role modeling and personal example.

Similar pictures can be envisaged with regard to civilian roles. For instance, there is a growing interest in the organizational literature in computer-supported co-operative work (CSCW) and computer-mediated group decision support systems (GDSS). Such technologies and arrangements are presented not only as technical means for overcoming distance barriers, but also as means for increasing participation of team members, decreasing status barriers, enabling greater focus on the task, reducing "groupthink", and increasing creativity (e.g. Sproull & Kiesler, 1991).

Computer-mediated technologies and group decision support systems may enhance some leadership capabilities, mainly those related to the transmission of information between leaders and members. They may reduce the distance between top-level managers and lower-levels members and enable both parties to communicate with each other more effectively. By and large, however, such arrangements tend to de-emphasize the role of leaders. To the extent that they retain any role for leaders, it seems to be a very limited and "cold" role, which emphasizes the cognitive elements and de-emphasizes the social, human, and emotional elements of leadership. It is not clear, for instance, whether is it possible to identify with a "virtual" leader, and what kind of trust can be developed in such a leader.

The three inter-related scenarios of disposable leaders, shared leadership, and teleleadership imply a diminishing role for leaders and leadership in emerging organizations. Such scenarios cannot be ignored as they are consistent with present-day technological and organizational developments. However, in the next section I argue that there are reasons to derive a very different scenario regarding the role of leadership in future organizations. I will submit that precisely because organizations become boundaryless and flexible, both the scope and the need for leadership are enlarged, and that far from becoming disposable, leadership becomes indispensable in the boundaryless organization.

AN ALTERNATIVE SCENARIO: WEAKENING
SITUATIONS REQUIRE STRONGER LEADERSHIP

The detailed form of future organizations may be unpredictable, or may vary considerably among industrial sectors, between organizations and even within organizations. However, in principle, all forms of "boundarylessness" and increased flexibility have a common meaning: When organizations become less bounded and more flexible, they function more like "weak situations" (Bell & Staw, 1989; Weick, 1996). The distinction between strong and weak situations was suggested by Mischel (1977). Strong situations lead everyone to construe the particular events in the same way, induce uniform expectations regarding the most appropriate response patterns, and require skills that everyone has to the same extent. Conversely, weak situations are not uniformly encoded, do not generate uniform expectations concerning the desired behaviour, and do not offer clear incentives contingent upon performance.

Bureaucratic organizations of the industrial era have been strong situations for their members. Fixed hierarchies, boundaries, and division of labour, rules, regulations, and standard ways of operation clearly define actors' roles, relationships and the expected consequences of behaviour and thus "strengthen" the situation from the organizational members' point of view. In contrast, the more the organization becomes flexible and boundaryless the more it becomes a weak situation by definition. Role ambiguity is high, relationships shift and consequences of action cannot always be predicted with a high degree of certainty.

The weakening of organizational situations has some very important implications for leadership in organizations. First, as the regulation of behaviour through rules, procedures, policies, and so on, becomes increasingly impossible, there emerges an increased scope and need for leadership. It is precisely under such weak circumstances that leadership, as opposed to management, becomes important. Since the organizational structure cannot be relied upon as the primary mechanism for achieving co-ordination, other means have to be employed for that purpose. In the absence of specific rules and fixed structures, people need mental models to help them handle the situations they face and coordinate their actions with each other. Even a temporary organization must provide its members with a mental framework that represents guiding principles for their behaviour.

It should be noted that the weakening of the situation includes not only the organizational structures but also the weakening of previously strong and unified organizational cultures. If only structures were weakening, co-ordination and control could be achieved by normative or "clan" control (Ouchi, 1980), namely by organizational cultures that instill in their members shared world views, shared values, and shared behavioural norms through the process of socialization (Kunda, 1992). However, achieving coordination by clan or culture control becomes increasingly difficult, if not impossible, in the boundaryless organization due to the frequently changing composition of organizational and interorganizational arrangements, that bring together for limited durations and specific projects members of different departmental, organizational, and often even national cultures.

When organizational structures and cultures are strong and stable, they may serve as "substitutes for leadership" (Kerr & Jermier, 1978). In the absence of stable structures and strong cultures, there are no substitutes for leadership, and leaders have to provide the mental models and frameworks to co-ordinate the behaviour of organizational members. The current emphasis in the leadership literature on "framing" (Fairhurst & Sarr, 1996) and "frame alignment" (Shamir, et al., 1993) reflects this recognition. Framing refers to leaders" influence on the meanings given to events by other people. It is through such influence on meanings that leaders motivate others, reinforce collective ties, and direct collective action.

The need for framing in weak organizational situations extends beyond the needs for work regulation or coordination. It applies to the more fundamental issues of purpose and meaning. Indeed, it has been shown (Barker, 1993) that self-managed teams can, under certain circumstances, develop a form of "concertive control" that replaces more than adequately the co-ordination and control functions of the supervisor. Presumably, one of the conditions for such effective team-based control is longevity and relative stability of team membership, an issue to be discussed in a later section. However, even in the highly co-ordinated self-managed team described by Barker (1993) the sense of purpose could not be found within the teams themselves, and had to be provided by the vision of a top-level leader.

DeFillippi and Arthur (1996), following Hall (1992), discuss three arenas of organizational competency: knowing why, knowing-how, and knowing-whom. The temporary, freelance, or even remote workers of boundaryless organizations may have the know-how. They may also be interconnected through occupational or industry-based networks, thus retaining the "knowing whom" competency. Therefore, the "knowing how" and "knowing whom" competencies may not reside in any particular organization. However, the "knowing why" competency reflects the identity of a particular organization or system. Being organization-specific or project-specific it cannot be as transferable as the "knowing how" and even the "knowing whom" competencies.

Leadership has always carried primary responsibility for providing meaning and purpose to members of a collectivity. Indeed, being able to provide answers to "why" questions was offered as one explanation for the attribution of charisma to leaders (Shils, 1965; see Shamir, 1991). However, this responsibility is likely to increase as organizations lose their boundaries. In bounded organizations, the knowing why competency may be carried by the organizational culture, and transmitted to newcomers through lengthy processes of formal and informal socialization (Schein, 1992). In the flexible and boundaryless organizations of the future, membership is likely to change often, and lengthy socialization processes may no longer be possible. Therefore, culture cannot serve as a "substitute for leadership" (Kerr & Jermier, 1978) in this regard. Infusing work with meaning and purpose is thus left to the leaders (Cascio, 1995).

This is a particularly challenging task for three reasons: First, perhaps paradoxically, at the same time that the traditional mechanisms for producing organizational commitment such as stability, socialization and strong cultures are weakening, the need for commitment on the part of organizational members increases. In strong situations, much of the behaviour of members is determined by hierarchical structures, reward structures, and normative frameworks. In weak situations behaviour is determined more by factors such as personality dispositions and self-concepts (Bell & Staw, 1989; Weick, 1996). Internalized commitment to the organization or the task is a personal attitude that may guide work behaviour. House (1995, pp. 411–412) explains:

> Because much twenty-first century work will be intellectual rather than physical, to observe, monitor, and control the processes and behaviour by which organizational members accomplish their tasks will be difficult if not impossible. As a result, a substantial proportion of organizational members will work without direct supervision. These individuals will be the key to organizational success— they will perform the organization's most important work, be in greatest demand, and not be easily replaceable. Because work will be predominantly nonroutine and intellectual, effective performers must adjust to variable role demands and engage in frequent problem solving. Consequently, individual initiative, motivation, and willingness to take personal responsibility for task accomplishment will primarily determine both the quality and quantity of nonroutine work.

A second paradox, and challenge for the leadership of boundaryless organizations, is that at the time that organizational members get out of "boxes" and of permanent membership in departments and units, the importance of teams for the successful performance of many work tasks increases (Ilgen, Major, Hollenbeck, & Sego, 1993). The problem or challenge stems from the fact that team performance depends, at least partially, on stability of membership and on development processes that take time. Time may be needed for members to acquaint themselves with each other, stabilize roles within the group, and develop interpersonal trust and a shared perception of team potency (Avolio et al., 1996; Guzzo, Yost, Campbell, & Shea, 1993).

Intra-group trust, team potency, and members' collectivistic motivation are related to members' identification with the group. Identification means that members regard the group's successes and failures as their own successes and failures (Ashforth & Mael, 1989; Shamir, 1990). When, as in boundaryless organizations, members belong to multiple teams and change team membership frequently, there is a lower likelihood that a strong identification with any team will develop naturally. Thus, the task of creating a team out of a diverse collection of individuals, and developing social identification among team members, becomes more challenging precisely at the time that it is more acutely needed. There does not seem to be any "substitute for leadership" in this area either.

Finally, the weakening of organizational situations implies that it becomes less possible for organizational leaders to rely on position-related bases of power. Formal leadership in bureaucratic organizations is performed within relatively stable formal patterns of authority, and is at least partially backed by "legitimate" power (French & Raven, 1959). In boundaryless, lateral, and flexible organizations, there are no permanent hierarchy structures, and leaders cannot rely on formal authority. They may often find themselves "in charge" of units and people who are not permanently under their authority and who have joined their units for a specific project, including members of other units and organizations. Even the titles of formally designated leaders may change from managers and directors to conveners, co-ordinators, and facilitators. Furthermore, as mentioned earlier, they may be expected to alternate leading and following on a regular basis. Under such conditions, leadership must be exercised through persuasion and example. Legitimate power has to be replaced by expert power and "referent" power, which stems from the leader's personal characteristics and behaviours, and involves emotional bonds of identification and trust between leaders and followers.

To summarize, boundaryless, flattened, flexible, project-based, and team-based organizations that employ temporary, externalized, and remote workers, whose tasks are more intellectual and less routine and cannot be controlled and co-ordinated by structure or direct supervision, need mechanisms of co-ordination through shared meaning systems, a shared sense of purpose, and high member commitment to shared values. Therefore, boundaryless organizations are likely to need strong leadership to perform the integrative functions. The main function of organizational leaders becomes that of being "centres of gravity" in the midst of weakening frameworks, and balancing the centrifugal forces exerted by loosely coupled structures, fragmented cultures, temporary membership, and technologies that increase the distance between leaders and members. Scholarly interest, both theoretical and empirical, should therefore focus on the processes by which leaders perform their crucial integrative functions.

Movable or disposable leaders are unlikely to serve as integrators or "centres of gravity". Handy (1989) foresees future organizations built around a loyal core of employees who develop deep organization-specific knowledge and company loyalty. This core will be supported by a host of peripherals with diverse, temporary, networked relations—not insiders yet not outsiders. If leaders are to serve the integrative function they cannot be part of the peripherals. They must be part of the stable core. Indeed, they may have to be at "the core of the core" and serve as its most central and defining element.

In the past, the workforce of many organizations was relatively stable, whereas managers changed frequently. We may witness the reversal of this pattern. Leaders may have to represent the struggle for continuity and stability in the midst of frequently changing people and technologies. This role of leaders as guardians of stability may be required not only in order to perform the integrative functions discussed previously, but also for other reasons to be discussed later.

THE LEADER'S SAFETY-PROVIDING ROLE

An emphasis on continuity and stability is required due to the need to provide a sense of safety in times of change. Change creates anxiety, and anxiety leads to rigidity and defensiveness, especially if the change implies some threat to the more basic sense of identity or integrity that the person or group feels. People resist change, or even deny the need for change, because of a lack of psychological safety. "The essence of psychological safety is that we can imagine a needed change without feeling a loss of integrity or identity. If the change I have to make threatens my whole self, I will deny the data and the need for change. Only if I can feel that I will retain my identity or my integrity as I learn something new or make a change, will I even be able to contemplate it" (Schein, 1992, p. 300).

The same phenomenon occurs at the organizational level. Organizations often fail to adapt or to learn because they do not have the required level of safety to do so. Evidence for the need for change accumulates but is either ignored, denied or rationalized. According to Schein (1992) it is the leader of the group or organization who has the responsibility to absorb or contain the anxiety that is unleashed when things do not work as they should or the future is uncertain. "The importance of visionary leadership can be understood in this context, in that the vision sometimes serves the function of providing the psychological safety that permits the organization to move forward" (p. 301). Leaders may not have the answer, but they must provide temporary stability and emotional reassurance while the answer is being worked out. This anxiety-containing function is especially relevant during periods of learning, when old habits must be given up before new ones are learned. Moreover, if the world is increasingly changing, such anxiety may be perpetuated, requiring learning leaders to assume a perpetual supportive role.

This argument can be illustrated by the case of the late Israeli Prime Minister, Itzhak Rabin. Prior to his assassination, Rabin was not considered a particularly charismatic leader. A sceptic and a pessimist by nature he was not an inspirational leader in the regular sense of this word. Furthermore, he did not have a vision. In a recent newspaper interview (Haaretz, 3rd March, 1997), former Minister Yossi Baylin, who had initiated the discussions that eventually led to the Oslo accord between Israel and the Palestine Liberation Organization, related that: "After his death I sat with Mrs. Leah Rabin [Rabin's wife] and said to her: If someone were to know what kind of a permanent solution Rabin had in mind, it could only be you. And she said: Look, I can't tell you. He was very pragmatic. He hated to deal with what will happen many years from now. He thought only about what is happening now and what is going to happen soon. As far as I know he did not have a very clear picture of what the permanent solution should look like." Thus, Rabin's leadership style would not have qualified as highly charismatic or transformational by commonly accepted criteria (Bass, 1985; Conger & Kanungo, 1988; House, 1977). Yet in the latter part of his life he was certainly a leader of a major transformation or change in the relationships between Israel and the Palestinians, as well as between Israel and Jordan, and in this sense was more transformational than many leaders whose leadership style matches the transformational style much closer.

A case in point is Rabin's friend and rival Shimon Peres. In contrast to Rabin, Peres enjoys a reputation of an intellectually stimulating and visionary leader. Taking into account political, economic, technological, and scientific trends, he has formulated and clearly articulated a vision of the New Middle East. A believer and an optimist by nature, Mr Peres' ideas are imaginative, creative and transcend the current circumstances. In fact, the Oslo discussions with the Palestinians were held under his auspices, and only later brought to Rabin's attention and approval. And yet the Labour party ousted Peres and elected Rabin as its leader before the 1992 general elections, a decision that proved to be a success when Rabin won the elections. Furthermore, when the helm returned to Peres after Rabin's assassination, he could not win electorate support in 1996, lost the general elections, and most likely ended his political career.

At least part of the reason for Rabin's unexpected success and Peres's unexpected failure in the role of a transformational leader must be associated with their differential ability to inspire confidence and trust and contain follower anxiety in times of change. Rabin's ability to instill confidence among followers did not stem from his vision or optimism. Rather, it stemmed from his reputation as a security-minded and risk-averted person. Paradoxically, therefore, it was his conservatism that enabled him to be a man of change. Peres, in contrast, could not inspire the same amount of trust and confidence precisely because he was perceived to be a man of change: too visionary, too future-oriented, and lacking that centre of gravity and safety that Rabin was able to provide. Although these examples are taken from the political leadership sphere, we believe their lessons are no less applicable to organizational leadership.

RIGIDITY IN THE SERVICE OF LEARNING AND CHANGE

A supporting reason for emphasizing continuity as a vehicle for promoting change is provided by March (1995) in an essay on the role of imagination in organizational adaptation. March talks about the importance of exploitation and exploration for organizational adaptation, and views the adaptation problem as that of balancing exploitation and exploration. Exploitation refers to the short-term improvements, refinement, routinization, and elaboration of existing ideas, paradigms, technologies, strategies, and knowledge. It emphasizes improving existing capabilities and technologies. Exploration refers to experimentation with new ideas, paradigms, technologies, strategies, and knowledge in the hope of finding alternatives that improve old ones.

Without a steady stream of exploratory efforts, adaptation fails. However, exploration becomes useful only if can be sustained long enough to expose its true values. New ideologies, forms, and practices need to be buffered from learning what is technically efficient and normatively legitimate long enough to explore alternative efficiencies and legitimacies and to transform understanding of what works. *"In many ways, therefore, the problematic element in adaptation through exploration is not organizational flexibility but stability"* (March, 1995, p. 436, my emphasis).

How do organizations achieve sufficient rigidity in form, strategies, and technologies to make the process work well? March's answer (1995, p. 437) is by imagination: "Imaginations of possible organizations are justified by their potential not for predicting the future (which is almost certainly small) but for nurturing the uncritical commitment and persevering madness required for sustained organizational and individual rigidity in a selective environment." March links these imaginations to the leader's vision and the overtones of dreams attached to this word. In other words, in contrast with the literature that emphasizes the role of visions in motivation and guiding change (e.g. Bennis & Nanus, 1985), March views the primary role of visions as that of motivating stability following exploration. This view, even if only partially true, reveals the potentially complex nature of the interrelationship between change and stability as they relate to leadership roles in unstable environments.

THEORETICAL CHALLENGES

Theories of leadership in the 1980s and 1990s have focused on "transforming", "transformational", "visionary", "inspirational", or "charismatic" leadership (Bass, 1985; Burns, 1978; House, 1977; Sashkin, 1988). Collectively, these theories have been referred to as "The New Leadership Theories" (Bryman, 1992) or "Neocharismatic Theories" (House, 1995), reflecting the fact that while there are differences of emphasis among the various theories, there are also many similarities, and together they can be seen to constitute a single genre or even a single paradigm (see also, Bass, 1996; House & Shamir, 1993; Yukl, 1994).

A central common characteristic of the New Leadership theories is an emphasis on the role of leaders as change agents. This emphasis is captured in the names given to the type of leadership discussed by the theories, which often include the verb "transform", as well as in some of the theories' dominant themes. These include a great emphasis on a proactive approach to the environment, dissatisfaction with the status quo, initiating change and innovation, and motivating and inspiring commitment to change among organizational members (Bryman, 1992, p. 111). According to Kotter, (1990, pp. 4–5) the fundamental difference between management and leadership (which to some extent parallels the distinction between "old" and "new" leadership) is that the former is concerned with activities which are designed to produce "consistency and order", whereas the latter is concerned with "constructive or adaptive change". Kanter et al. (1991) regard responding to change, harnessing change, and creating change as the major leadership challenges.

In a similar vein, theories of charismatic and visionary leadership (Conger & Kanungo, 1988; Sashkin, 1988) emphasize the importance of leader sensitivity to the environment and adaptability to changing circumstances. The emphasis on the transforming function of leaders in the New Leadership theories is perhaps particularly evident in the role given by these theories to the leader's vision. The vision is seen as the main vehicle for articulating and presenting an image of a better future, and for motivating and guiding the organization and its members towards such a future (e.g. Bennis & Nanus, 1985).

However, the emphasis on the role of leaders as change agents has led to a neglect of their role as "centres of gravity" and agents of continuity. This neglect may reflect a tendency in parts of the management literature to endow change with a positive value and to idealize change for its own sake (Bryman, 1992). It may also be traced back to the origins of the New Leadership theories in Weber's original notion of charisma. Weber (1924/1947) saw societal order as explained by traditional and rational-legal bases of authority, and introduced the leader's charisma as a third base of authority to explain how and why people are willing to follow a leader who intends to change the normative order of society. According to Weber, the attribution of special qualities to the leader enables followers to trust the leader sufficiently to overcome their fear of change and resistance to change.

In the Weberian framework charisma and change are strongly interrelated. Charisma is a relatively temporary and short–lived phenomenon. All charisma has to be routinized and institutionalized eventually (Trice & Beyer, 1986). Organizational rules and cultural norms must replace the charisma of the leader, and the charismatic authority has to be replaced by traditional and bureaucratic authority in order to stabilize the system after the transformation.

The Weberian concept of charisma as characterizing infrequent periods of radical change was appropriate for more stable times. For present-day organizations such a concept is no longer useful. The growing rate of environmental and technological change and the emergence of boundaryless organizations have two implications that are difficult to reconcile with each other within the Weberian framework: On the one hand, due to increased ambiguity and the weakening of structures and permanent cultures, the need for charisma in the sense of meaning-giving and safety-providing leadership grows. On the other hand, in the "post-bureaucratic" and "post-organizational-culture" age institutionalization of charisma becomes increasingly difficult. How can charisma be institutionalized if it cannot be replaced by a bureaucratic or a normative order? Indeed, the very nature of the boundaryless organization reflects the second implication, because, in such an organization, "Many of the new activity sets are only minimally institutionalized. They do not exist or persist irrespective of the people occupying them" (Kanter et al., 1991, p. 13).

Therefore, here lies a major practical and theoretical challenge: As change becomes a permanent feature of organizational life rather than an infrequent occurrence, charisma, in the sense of meaning-giving leadership and strong trusting relationships between leaders and members, becomes increasingly necessary for effective organizational adaptation and action. However, if charisma can no longer be institutionalized and replaced by structural or normative arrangements, how can it be maintained?

We need a concept of charisma for our times—neither temporary nor institutionalized. Such charisma may be less dramatic than the original concept. It does not have to include the perception of the leader as extraordinary or the attribution of super-human qualities to the leader. Charisma may not even be an appropriate term for such leadership. Yet we need a model of strong enough referent power to explain how leaders perform the integrative functions, offer answers to "why" questions, increase members' internalized commitment, and provide the psychological safety needed in times of change, all this without the support of permanent structures, strong cultures, or other "substitutes". Furthermore, we need a model that focuses on leaders' ability to balance or synthesize contradictory role requirements (Hooijberg, Hung, & Dodge, 1997), as it has to explain how leaders can simultaneously serve the seemingly contradictory functions of providing stability, which is required for integration, learning and safety, and facilitating change, which is required for adaptation to the environment.

IDENTITY-BASED LEADERSHIP

An appropriate theory of leadership for the post-bureaucratic and boundaryless organization has not been developed yet. In the final section of this article I suggest that the concept of identity could be a pivotal element in such a theory due to its capacity to contain and reconcile a strong emphasis on continuity with a strong emphasis on change. Organizational or group identity describes what people define as central, distinctive, and enduring about their organization or group (Albert & Whetten, 1985). It has been shown that identities provide a sense of meaning and purpose, provide justifications for individual and collective action, and serve as schema for the interpretation of events (Dutton & Dukerich, 1991; Dutton, Dukerich, & Harquail, 1994).

It has been less emphasized in the organizational literature, however, that identities are not totally fixed. Anthropological studies have shown that identities are continuously produced by individual and collective social actors who constitute and transform themselves through their practices and relations (Mato, 1996). From this perspective, identities are better understood not merely as something that people "have", but also as something that people do (Friedman, 1996). It has been suggested that leadership, particularly charismatic leadership, often plays a central role both in framing action in terms of collective identities, and in reframing the identities themselves (Shamir, Arthur, & House, 1994; Shamir et al., 1993).

The self-concept based motivational theory of charismatic leadership (Shamir et al., 1993) can serve as a basis for the development of a more complete identity-based theory of leadership. While the theory focuses on charismatic leaders, it is in fact a more general theory of referent power. It suggests that referent power is based on the leader's ability to harness the self-concept related motivations of followers, or more specifically the motivational forces of self-expression, self-consistency, self-esteem, and self-worth. Leaders harness these motivations by their verbal and symbolic behaviours, which raise the salience of certain values and identities in followers' self-concepts, and by articulating the goals and required efforts in terms of these values and identities, thus linking them to valued aspects of followers' self-concepts. Consequently, the goals and efforts become more meaningful for followers who develop internalized commitment to these goals.

Shamir et al. (1993) argue that strong internalized commitment is in the final analysis commitment to a certain concept of self. Therefore, it is a function of the extent to which individuals identify with their organizations or units, and with the values for which their organizations or leaders stand, and the extent to which they experience self-consistency and self-worth contingent on their contributions to the organization and its goals.

The most crucial aspects of the self-concepts highlighted by Shamir et al.'s theory are those that link the individual to the collectivity: values and identities. The theory de-emphasizes personal identification with the leader in the psychoanalytic sense (which is also consistent with Weber's charisma) of identifying with an infantile father figure. It emphasizes social identification with the collectivity, and regards personal identification with the leader as primarily identification with the leader as a representative character and symbol of the group. The emphasis on values and identities and on social identification processes provide the basis for the leader's social integration role.

One of the motivational mechanisms posited by Shamir et al. (1993) is the mechanism of self-consistency. A sense of self-consistency depends, among other things, on a perception of continuity of the self between the past, the present, and the anticipated or hoped for future. Self-consistency in this sense does not mean stagnation and rejection of change, but an experience of "evolving", which makes present actions and future goals meaningful in terms of the past. Shamir et al., therefore, explicitly hypothesized that the motivational effect of leaders, and the appeal of their visions and missions to others, rest in part on the leaders' ability to make the required efforts and future goals more meaningful for followers by connecting them to the collective history, traditions, heroes, etc.

From the perspective of this theory it can be argued that, contrary to what is implied by Weber's classification, charismatic authority and traditional authority are no opposites. In fact, in many cases charisma has been explicitly based on tradition. The Ayatollah Khomeini is an obvious example (Fisher, 1980). But even in less extreme and less explicit cases, charismatic leaders often reject tradition and embrace tradition at the same time. This is possible because identities and self-concepts often contain both a desire for continuity and a desire for change.

Indeed, there is some evidence that leaders are able to simultaneously emphasize both change and continuity. For instance, an unpublished content-analysis of US Presidents' inaugural addresses conducted with a group of graduate students in a research seminar, has revealed both a strong emphasis on change and a strong emphasis on tradition, history, and continuity in most speeches. Examples of such a dual emphasis can also be found in a published content-analysis of a speech by Jesse Jackson (Shamir et al., 1994).

However, identities depend on boundaries, since they are defined by individuals and social collectivities in relation to a larger social context (Fiol, 1991). Therefore, "identification implies boundary making insofar as that which is identified can be perceived, recognized, distinguished from its surroundings" (Friedman, 1996, p. 129). Boundaryless organizations, interorganizational networks and ad hoc project groups do not have clear boundaries by definition. It follows that if leaders are to serve as "centres of gravity" in boundaryless organizations, provide the necessary integrative functions and endow collective action with a sense of meaning and purpose, and if they are to do so primarily through the consolidation of identities, their main role may be to enact symbolic boundaries for the group in order to replace the collapsing physical and structural boundaries. In a similar vein, Hirschhorn and Gilmore (1992) have argued that as traditional boundaries of hierarchy, function, and geography disappear, a new set of boundaries, primarily psychological, becomes important in organizations. Therefore, they argued that leaders in flexible organizations must focus on the management of these psychological boundaries, among them the identity boundary.

This clearly implies that the role of the leader in boundaryless organizations is more than a convener, co-ordinator of facilitator role. It implies "invention" of identities through rhetoric devices such as slogans and metaphors, production of artifacts symbolizing group identity, interpretation of tasks and actions in terms of identities, and symbolic control of group membership through rites of entry to and exit from the group. It further implies the capacity of the leaders himself or herself to serve as a symbol of the collective identity. This capacity depends on the leader's biography, values, personal behaviours, and the way he or she presents him- or herself to members of the group and to outsiders. However, since identities cannot be imposed on people, nor can they be invented from scratch, the leader's ability to consolidate an identity for the group and serve as a representative character of that identity depends no less on members' biographies, values, and existing identities.

IN CONCLUSION

In this article, I examined certain trends in the organizational sphere, and their implications for the kind of leadership that is likely to be needed and to emerge in more flexible and boundaryless organizations. My characterization of the new organizational forms has been crude. Not all organizations and organizational units are becoming boundaryless or de-bureaucratized. Indeed, there are also opposite trends. For instance, some developments in information and tele-communication technologies may facilitate the enforcement of standard operating procedures, and enable managers to exert greater control on the performance of workers at all levels. Thus, they may represent a reduction in flexibility, and a trend toward bureaucratization rather than de-bureaucratization.

Furthermore, my discussion has been crude in the sense that it has not distinguished among types of organization, types of task, and levels of leadership. Obviously, my arguments would apply differentially to various circumstances and leadership roles. However, I believe the trends examined here are prevalent enough to warrant attention from leadership scholars and practitioners at all levels. The weakening of bureaucratic structures and boundaries can be observed in many organizations. Indeed, they have even reached that archetype of bureaucratic organizations, the military, as evidenced, for instance, by a recent collection of essays on military leadership in the 21st century, which is entitled *Out of the Box Leadership* (Hunt, Dodge, & Wong, 1999). Therefore, it seemed appropriate, for analytical purposes, to start the analysis of recent organizational trends and their implications for leadership theory and practice, by trying to identify the common denominators of the various trends, portray an "ideal type" of a boundaryless organization, and examine the leadership challenges and needs in such an organization. Hopefully, further theoretical analysis and empirical studies will allow us to fine-tune our arguments, specify the limits of their applicability, and distinguish more clearly among types of organizations and tasks, and among roles and levels of leadership.

Meanwhile, our preliminary analysis has led to the tentative conclusion that in post-bureaucratic, fragmentary, and boundaryless organizations the main challenges facing organizational leadership will be to: (1) replace weakening organizational structures and cultures with coherent frameworks or mental models in order to enable co-ordinated collective action; (2) increase commitment among members when such commitment is increasingly needed due to the changing nature of work; (3) create and maintain teams and teamwork despite the diversity and fluidity of membership in teams and organizational units; (4) provide a sense of psychological safety in order to counteract members' anxieties due to increased uncertainty rate of change; and (5) support a degree of stability and persistence needed for individual and organizational learning.

It is unlikely that any form of weak or disposable leadership will be able to meet these challenges. Nor is it likely that strong substitutes for leadership will be found in these areas. The above–mentioned challenges imply leadership that can simultaneously and strongly emphasize both continuity and change, and can establish and maintain collective identities in the absence of traditional identity–forming boundaries. The need to capture such contradictions and complexities in a single conception of leadership presents leadership scholars with a major theoretical challenge.

REFERENCES

Albert, S., & Whetten, D.A. (1985). Organizational identity. In L.L. Cummings & B.M. Staw (Eds.), *Research in organizational behaviour, Vol. 7* (pp. 263–295). Greenwich, CT: JAI Press.

Arthur, M.B., & Rousseau, D.M. (1996). Conclusion: A lexicon for the new organizational era. In M.B. Arthur & D.M. Rousseau (Eds.), *The boundaryless career: A new employment principle for a new organizational era.* New York: Oxford University Press.

Ashforth, B.E., & Mael, F. (1989). Social identity theory and the organization. *Academy of Management Review, 14*(1), 20–39.

Avolio, B.J, Jung, D.J., Murry, W., & Sivasubramaniam, N. (1996). Building highly developed teams: Focusing on shared leadership processes, efficacy, trust and performance. *Advances in interdisciplinary studies of work teams, 3*, 173–209. Greenwich, CT: JAI Press.

Barker, J.R. (1993). Tightening the iron cage: Concertive control in self-managing teams. *Administrative Science Quarterly, 38*, 408–437.

Barker, R.A. (1997). How can we train leaders if we do not know what leadership is? *Human Relations, 50*(4), 343–362.

Bass, B.M. (1985). *Leadership and performance beyond expectations.* New York: The Free Press.

Bass, B.M. (1996). *A new paradigm of leadership: An inquiry into transformational leadership.* Alexandria, VA: US Army Research Institute for the Behavioural and Social Science.

Bell, N.E., & Staw, B.M. (1989). People as sculptors versus sculpture: The roles of personality and personal control in organizations. In M.B. Arthur, D.T. Hall, & B.S. Lawrence (Eds.), *Handbook of career theory.* New York: Cambridge University Press.

Bennis, W.G., & Nanus, B. (1985). *Leaders: The strategies for taking charge.* New York: Harper & Row.

Bryman, A. (1992). *Charisma and leadership in organizations.* London: Sage.

Burns, J.M. (1978). *Leadership.* New York: Harper & Row.

Burns, J.M. (1996, September). *Empowerment for change: A conceptual working paper.* Paper presented to the Kellog Leadership Studies Project, University of Maryland.

Cascio, W.F. (1995). Whither industrial and organizational psychology in a changing world of work? *American Psychologist, 50*(11), 928–939.

Conger, J.A., & Kanungo, R.N. (1988). Behavioural dimensions of charismatic leadership. In J.A. Conger & R.N. Kanungo (Eds.), *Charismatic leadership: The elusive factor in organizational effectiveness.* San Francisco: Jossey-Bass.

Davidow, W., & Malone, M. (1992). *The virtual corporation.* New York: Harper Collins.

Davis, D.D. (1995). Form, function and strategy in boundaryless organizations. In A. Howard (Ed.), *The changing nature of work.* San Francisco: Jossey-Bass.

DeFillippi, R.J., & Arthur, M.B. (1996). Boundaryless contexts and careers: A competency-based perspective. In M.B. Arthur & D.M. Rousseau (Eds.), *The boundaryless career: A new employment principle for a new organizational era.* New York: Oxford University Press.

Dutton, J.E., & Dukerich, J.M. (1991). Keeping an eye on the mirror: The role of image and identity in organizational adaptation. *Academy of Management Journal, 34,* 517–554.

Dutton, J.E., Dukerich, J.M., & Harquail, C.V. (1994). Organizational images and member identification. *Administrative Science Quarterly, 39,* 239–263.

Fairhurst, G.T., & Sarr, R.A. (1996). *The art of framing: Managing the language of leadership.* San Francisco: Jossey–Bass.

Fiol, C.M. (1991). Managing culture as a competitive resource: An identity-based view of sustainable competitive advantage. *Journal of Management, 17*(1), 191–211.

Fisher, M.M.J. (1980). Becoming Mullah: Reflections on Iranian clerics in a revolutionary age. *Iranian Studies, 13,* 1–4.

French, J.R.P., & Raven, B. (1959). The bases of social power. In D. Cartwright (Ed.), *Studies in social power.* Ann Arbor, MI: University of Michigan, Institute of Social Research.

Friedman, J. (1996). The politics of de-authentification: Escaping from identity. *Identities, 3*(1–2), 127–136.

Gemmil, G., & Oakley, J. (1992). Leadership: An alienating social myth? *Human Relations, 45,* 113–129.

Guzzo, R.A., Yost, P.R., Campbell, R.J., & Shea, G.P. (1993). Potency in groups: Articulating a construct. *British Journal of Social Psychology, 32,* 87–106.

Hall, R. (1992). The strategic analysis of intangible resources. *Strategic Management Journal, 13,* 135–144.

Handy, C. (1989). *The age of unreason.* Cambridge, MA: Harvard Business School Press.

Hecksher, C., & Donnellon, A. (Eds.). (1994). *The post-bureaucratic organization: New perspectives on organizational change.* Thousand Oaks, CA: Sage.

Hirschhorn, L., & Gilmore, T. (1992). The new boundaries of the "boundaryless" company. *Harvard Business Review, 70*(5/6), 104–115.

Hooijberg, R., Hunt, J.G., & Dodge, G.E. (1997). Leadership complexity and development of the leaderplex model. *Journal of Management, 23,* 375–408.

House, R.J. (1977). A 1976 theory of charismatic leadership. In J.G. Hunt & L.L. Larson (Eds.), *Leadership: The cutting edge.* Carbondale, IL: Southern Illinois University Press.

House, R.J. (1995). Leadership in the twenty-first century: A speculative inquiry. In A. Howard (Ed.), *The changing nature of work.* San Francisco: Jossey-Bass.

House, R.J., & Adytia, R. (1997). *The social scientific study of leadership: Quo vadis.* Unpublished manuscript. The Wharton School of Management, University of Pennsylvania.

House, R.J., & Shamir, B. (1993). Toward the integration of transformational, charismatic and visionary theories. In M.M. Chemers & R. Ayman (Eds.), *Leadership theory and research: Perspectives and directions.* Orlando, FL: Academic Press.

Hunt, J.G., Dodge, G.E., & Wong, L. (Eds.). (1999). *Out of the box leadership: Transforming the 21st century army and other top-performing organizations.* Stanford, CA: JAI Press.

Ilgen, D.R., Major, D.A., Hollenbeck, J.R., & Sego, D.J. (1993). Team research in the 1990s. In M.M. Chemers & R. Ayman (Eds.), *Leadership theory and research: Perspectives and directions.* Orlando, FL: Academic Press.

Kanter, R.M., Stein B.A., & Jick, T.D. (1991). *The challenge of organizational change: How companies experience it and leaders guide it*. New York: The Free Press.

Kerr, S., & Jermier, J. (1978). Substitutes for leadership: Their meaning and measurement. *Organizational Behaviour and Human Performance*, 22, 374–403.

Kotter, J.P. (1990). *A force for change: How leadership is different from management*. New York: Free Press.

Kunda, G. (1992). *Engineering culture*. Philadelphia: Temple University Press.

Manz, C.C., & Sims, H.P., Jr. (1993). *Business without bosses: How self-managing teams are building high performance companies*. New York: Wiley.

March, J.G. (1995). The future, disposable organizations and the rigidities of imagination. *Organization*, 2, 427–440.

Mato, D. (1996). On the theory, epistemology, and politics of the social construction of "cultural identities" in the age of globalization. *Identities*, 3(1–2), 61–67.

McCall, M.W., Jr., & Lombardo, M.M. (1978). *Leadership: Where else can we go?* Durham, NC: Duke University Press.

Meindl, J.R. (1990). On leadership: An alternative to the conventional wisdom. In B.M. Staw & L.L. Cummings (Eds.), *Research in organizational behaviour, Vol. 12* (pp. 159–203). Greenwich, CT: JAI Press.

Meindl, J.R., Ehrlich, S.B., & Dukerich, J.M. (1985). The romance of leadership. *Administrative Science Quarterly*, 30, 78–102.

Miner, J.B. (1975). The uncertain future of the leadership concept. In J.G. Hunt & L.L. Larson (Eds.), *Leadership frontiers*. Kent, OH: Kent State University Press.

Mischel, W. (1977). The interaction of person and situations. In D. Magnusson & N. Endler (Eds.), *Personality at the crossroads*. Hillsdale, NJ: Lawrence Erlbaum Associates Inc.

Mohrman, S.A., & Cohen, S.G. (1995). When people get out of the box: New relationships, new systems. In A. Howard (Ed.), *The changing nature of work*. San Francisco: Jossey-Bass.

Ouchi, W.G. (1980). Markets, bureaucracies and clans. *Administrative Science Quarterly*, 25, 129–141.

Sashkin, M. (1988). The visionary leader. In J.A. Conger & R.N. Kanungo (Eds.), *Charismatic leadership: The elusive factor in organizational effectiveness*. San Francisco: Jossey-Bass.

Schein, E.H. (1992). *Organizational culture and leadership*, (2nd ed.). San Francisco: Jossey-Bass.

Shamir, B. (1990). Calculations, values and identities: The sources of collectivistic work motivation. *Human Relations*, 43, 313–332.

Shamir, B. (1991). The charismatic relationship: Alternative explanations and predictions. *Leadership Quarterly*, 2, 81–104.

Shamir, B., Arthur, M.B., & House, R.J. (1994). The rhetoric of charismatic leadership: A theoretical extension, a case study and implications for research. *Leadership Quarterly*, 5(1), 25–42.

Shamir, B., & Ben-Ari, E. (1999). Leadership in an open army? Civilian connections, interorganizational frameworks, and changes in military leadership. In J.G. Hunt, G.E. Dodge & L. Wong (Eds.), *Out-of-the-box leadership: Transforming the twenty-first century army and other top-performing organizations* (pp. 15–40). Stanford, CT: JAI Press.

Shamir, B., House, R.J., & Arthur, M.B. (1993). The motivational effects of charismatic leadership: A self-concept based theory. *Organization Science*, 4, 577–594.

Shils, E.A. (1965). Charisma, order and status. *American Sociological Review*, 30, 199–213.

Sproull, L., & Kiesler, S. (1991). *Connections: New ways of working in the networked world*. Cambridge, MA: MIT Press.

Trice, H.M., & Beyer, J.M. (1986). Charisma and routinization in two social movement organizations. In B.M. Staw & L.L. Cummings (Eds.), *Research in organizational behaviour. Vol. 8* (pp. 113–164). Greenwich, CT: JAI Press.

Weber, M. (1947). *The theory of social and economic organization*. New York: Free Press. (Original work published 1924).

Weick, K.E. (1996). Enactment and the boundaryless career: Organizing as we work. In M.B. Arthur & D.M. Rousseau (Eds.), *The boundaryless career: A new employment principle for a new organizational era*. New York: Oxford University Press.

Yukl, G. (1994). *Leadership in organizations* (3rd ed.). Englewood Cliffs, NJ: Prentice-Hall.

EUROPEAN JOURNAL OF WORK AND ORGANIZATIONAL PSYCHOLOGY, 1999, 8 (1), 73–85

Role-playing and Attitude Change:
How Helping Your Boss can Change
the Meaning of Work

John B. Rijsman

*Faculty of Social Sciences, Department of Psychology,
Tilburg University, The Netherlands*

This article shows how the classic research paradigm of role-playing and attitude change (e.g. Festinger & Carlsmith, 1959), can better be used to demonstrate how the structural relation between leader and follower (i.e. between experimenter and subject) influences the follower's evaluation of work (i.e. of the subject's evaluation of the experimental task), than to demonstrate how the content of the played role influences the subsequent attitude of the subject. This is done by a gradual unmasking of the attitudinal approach as a rhetorical device, and by showing step by step how the structural approach is more powerful to explain the results. The final conclusion is that free role-playing is actually an implementation of the subject's a priori desire to collaborate with the leader (i.e. the experimenter) and which, via the co-ownership of work that it creates, induces a less negative and eventually even a more positive attitude towards the experimental work that needs to be done (or towards work-related aspects of the institution in which that work needs to be done).

INTRODUCTION

Experiments about role-playing and attitude change, such as for example Festinger and Carlsmith (1959), and several other experiments of the same kind (e.g. Elms, 1969), are usually described in the literature as experiments about how the verbal content of the played role influences the subsequent attitude of the role-playing subject. Many different theories are proposed on how this happens, varying from dissonance reduction, over learning, to a purely acognitive contagion of evaluative responses (e.g. Nuttin, 1974). However, when we look carefully at the design and the procedures of these experiments, we see that role-playing is typically induced by asking the subject to assist the experimenter in his or her own work (e.g. to act as a substitute for a sick assistant in order to help to

Requests for reprints should be addressed to J.B. Rijsman, Faculty of Social Sciences, Dept. of Psychology, Tilburg University, PO Box 90153, 5000 LE Tilburg, The Netherlands; email: j.b.rijsman@kub.nl manipulate the next subject), and that the dependent measure of the so-called attitude is typically a measure of how the subject evaluates that work, or at least some aspect of the institution in which the experimental work is performed. Therefore, we can also, perhaps for the better, look at these experiments as manipulations of the institutional or structural relationship between leader and followers (i.e. experimenter and subjects), and at the results as illustrations of how this relationship influences the followers' evaluation of the institutional work (e.g. the pleasantness of the experimental task, the quality of other work-related aspects of the institution). That is what we will try to do in this article.

First, we will review some of the most classic experiments in this tradition, and demonstrate how the traditional description of these experiments as experiments on how the verbal content of the played role influences the attitude of the subject is actually a rhetorical misrepresentation of facts. Second, we will look carefully at the structural dimension of these experiments, and show how this structural dimension is probably a better candidate for an explanation of what has been found. Third, we will demonstrate directly how a manipulation of the structural dimension, which is usually connected to the induction of verbal role-playing, is in itself a sufficient condition to induce the same kind of changes in the subjects' evaluation of the experimental work as the ones which are usually (but as shown earlier, inappropriately) attributed to the verbal content of the played role. Finally, we will look again at a couple of experiments on verbal role-playing, but now explicitly combined with structural variations, and observe that structure, and not content, is the most dominant factor in explaining the results. In that same context, however, we will also observe that content can become very important for people who are not really involved in the experiment (because they did not really perform the experimental task), so that what they say about the experiment is indeed an outsider's rhetorical construction of it (or precisely the position of authors of articles and textbooks, who also write about these experiments as outsiders, and thus describe them in contentual terms). To conclude, we will try to draw some lessons from these experiments about the role of leadership and the followers' evaluation of work in general.

THE CLASSIC INTERPRETATION OF THE FESTINGER AND CARLSMITH (1959) ROLE-PLAYING EXPERIMENT, AND THE RHETORICAL MYTH OF A CONTENTUAL EFFECT

In the rhetorical description of the classic Festinger and Carlsmith (1959) experiment in the literature, we always read that subjects who have performed an unpleasant experimental task, and who then freely (or actually for one dollar) help the experimenter by telling the next subject that it was pleasant, change their own attitude about the experimental task and start to think themselves that indeed it was pleasant. The reason this experiment is rhetorically described in this way is because it has to serve as an experimental demonstration of the fact that people in general cannot live with conscious contradictions in their own mind (or with cognitive dissonance, as Festinger and Carlsmith call this), so that when they contradict themselves, and cannot invoke sufficient external pressure (high rewards and so on) to justify what they did, they may change their attitude in the direction of what they said, to so reduce the cognitive dissonance.

However, at closer inspection, this rhetorical description of the Festinger and Carlsmith experiment is neither correct nor complete. To begin with, the experimental task of which the rhetorical description is always that it was unpleasant, was never judged unpleasant by subjects who actually performed the task. Indeed, Festinger and Carlsmith's control subjects (subjects who only performed the task and then told immediately how much they liked it or not) rated it, on a scale from –5 (very unpleasant) to +5 (very pleasant), on average –0.45, or in other words completely neutral (less than 5% away from the mid-point of the 11-point scale). And second, yes, the experimental subjects (those who for one dollar helped the experimenter by telling the next subject that it was pleasant), rated the task afterwards as somewhat more positive, namely +1.35, but nobody can tell for sure that this more positive rating was due to the positive content of the played role, for this content was not independently varied.

To control for the actual impact of the verbal content of the played role, Nuttin (1966) replicated the low reward conditions of Festinger and Carlsmith, but in one replication he let the subjects play a positive role, whereas in another replication he let them play a negative role. To his own astonishment, he did not find any difference between these two replications at all. Concretely, his positive-role subjects rated the task –0.45, or exactly neutral, as with the control subjects of Festinger and Carlsmith, and his negative-role subjects rated it +0.40, or paradoxically somewhat more positive than the positive-role subjects, but essentially neutral as well. His control subjects, again, also rated the task essentially neutral, at –0.90. For a remarkable reason, however, these essentially neutral results of Nuttin are virtually never mentioned in textbooks, so that, nearly four decades after the first publication of Festinger and Carlsmith, students in social psychology still learn that it was a good experimental demonstration of the fact that subjects who without (strong) external pressure lie about what they know, and tend to believe their own lie. And of course, in some sense it really is.

A NEW CONTENTUAL INTERPRETATION OF THE ROLE-PLAYING EFFECTS, BUT IN ACOGNITIVE TERMS

In his later work on experimental role-playing, Nuttin (1974) did no longer speak of a cognitive change of attitude, but of an acognitive contagion of evaluative responses. Concretely, he concluded that subjects who are highly aroused and who repeatedly express the same evaluative responses during role-playing (obviously positive ones in positive role-playing and negative ones in negative role-playing), tend to use more or less the same evaluative responses on the rating immediately after the role and, once they have done that, also on repeated ratings much later. However, when the subjects are not highly aroused and/or when the first rating is not taken immediately after the role, this acognitive assimilation of evaluative responses, or "response contagion" as Nuttin calls this, does not take place.

This new acognitive interpretation of role-playing is obviously also contentual in nature (the evaluative responses in the role determine, at least under the appropriate conditions of arousal and temporal contiguity, those on the rating), but unfortunately this is not exactly, or at least not literally what Nuttin found. What Nuttin concretely found was this. Students at the Catholic University of Leuven and Louvain-la-Neuve, who all despised their conservative exam system (control subjects rated it, on a scale from 1 (very negative) to 17 (very positive), on an average of 2.3), were asked to either defend (positive role) or attack (negative role) the system, in either normal (low arousal) or abnormal (high arousal) circumstances. By abnormal circumstances in this case, we must under-stand circumstances in which the experimenter (a well-known female professor at the University), acted completely out of role toward the student-subjects (e.g. by dressing provocatively, by blaming them without reason, by paying them too much or too little, etc.). It was found that in the normal condition (the condition in which the experimenter acted as a normal professor), the content of the played role had no differential effect at all, both the positive- and the negative-role subjects rated the exam system afterwards around 4.5, i.e. somewhat less negatively than the control subjects. In the abnormal condition, however, the verbal content of the played role had a dramatic effect: The negative-role subjects rated the system 1.8, i.e. more negative than the already very negative control subjects, whereas the positive-role subjects rated it completely neutral (around 8.0).

However, Nuttin interpreted these neutral ratings as symptoms of an acognitive response assimilation to the positive responses in the preceding role. But obviously that is not really the case, for neutral is not a response that bears any acognitive resemblance to positive, or in any case not more than to negative. Only if we interpret 8.0 as closer to positive than 2.3, can we say that it represents a shift in the positive direction, but that shift is not an acognitive assimilation of evaluative responses, just like a rating of orange, on a scale from yellow to red, after role-playing red, is not an acognitive assimilation to red either (despite our understanding that orange is a chemical mixture of yellow and red).

Since there was not a literal acognitive assimilation of evaluative responses in at least one of the crucial conditions of Nuttin, we can as well look for another (and in this case more structural) interpretation of what Nuttin really found. For example, an interpretation in which we say that the students who were confronted with an anti-conservative professor who nevertheless wanted them to defend the conservative exam system, did not precisely know what to say, and thus responded neutral instead of anything else. Students in the negative abnormal condition, who were confronted with an anti-conservative professor who also wanted them to attack the conservative exam system, probably felt safer, if not stimulated, to express their typical student-like rejection of the system, i.e. 1.8 instead of 2.3. In the normal condition, however, this function of confirmation or disconfirmation of the changed structural identity of the professor (and by implication also of the student in relation to that professor) could not take place, because this structural identity was not changed in the first place. The only shift in structural relationship between student and experimenter that probably took place in that situation was that the students, by freely helping their normal professor in her normal work (e.g. the doing of research), felt closer to this professor than before, and thus mitigated a bit their typical rejection of the exam system (or an aspect of the professor–student relationship that is defended by normal professors).

However, whatever the merits of this tentative reinterpretation of Nuttin's results in structural terms (or terms in which also the content of the requested role has implications for the structural identity of subject and experimenter), we must say that the literal definition of response contagion was not confirmed by later experiments either. For example, Verhaeghe (1976) found that subjects rated an experimental task as less unpleasant, not only after having role-played pleasant attitudes about the task, but also after having role-played interesting or worthwhile attitudes about it, or in other words the precise nature of the evaluative responses in the played role did not seem of any importance at all.

Poiesz (1977), in an attempt to verify the crucial role of acognitive arousal, did not find the predicted effects either. Concretely, he asked drugged subjects (drugged with valerian, inducing low arousal, or with caffeine, inducing high arousal) to play either a positive (positive condition) or a negative (negative condition) role about an issue, or to play no role at all (control condition). He found that, independent of the level of arousal, the control subjects rated the issue afterwards around 3.5 (on a scale from 1 to 11), the negative-role subjects about 4.0, and the positive-role subjects about 5.5. Thus, there was no interaction at all between arousal and content, and the high arousal negative subjects rated the issue even less (instead of more) negative than the control subjects, and the high arousal positive subjects, again, rated the issue neutral (instead of literally positive).

A MORE STRUCTURAL INTERPRETATION OF THE ATTITUDINAL EFFECT OF EXPERIMENTAL ROLE-PLAYING

Given these and many other examples of a non-verbatim (in the sense of not a literal reappearance of the role-responses in the rating-responses) effect of verbal role-playing, we decided to leave the issue of content aside for a while, and to look more carefully at the structural aspects of verbal role-playing. Concretely, we felt that merely asking the subject to help the experimenter in his or her own work as a researcher might have been enough to induce attitudes toward the experimental work, which are typically attributed to the content of the verbal role (but which, as shown already, can appear as well with positive as with negative role-playing). Apart from the obvious absence of a straightforward verbatim effect of role-playing in the cited experiments, we also felt attracted to this structural approach, because in our previous research on social hierarchization and competition (e.g. Rijsman, 1970, 1974, 1983a) we had theorized and found that subjects tend to compare themselves favourably with others, and that one particularly good method to do this is to identify themselves with others in the situation who already possess a superior status (such as experimenters in an experiment, obviously). Thus, we felt that subjects who were given an explicit opportunity to show solidarity with the experimenter by freely helping him or her in the experiment took this opportunity with both hands, and therefore rated the experiment less negative.

However, instead of speculating too long about all the possible identifications with the experimenter in verbal role-playing, and the possible consequences of these identifications for the subject's re-evaluation of the experimental work, we opted for a more direct strategy, and decided to run an experiment in which we would only manipulate the structural relationship between subject and experimenter, which is typically connected to the induction of verbal role-playing, but without any verbal role-playing at all. If we would find that only this structural manipulation would induce the same kind of evaluations as we typically find with verbal role-playing, we would obviously no longer need the verbal content to explain the results, and the door for a more structural interpretation of verbal role-playing would be wide open.

The first experiment that we ran in this line of research was as follows. We invited the subjects to the laboratory with the cover-story that we wanted to investigate the effects of conditioning on communication. When they arrived in the lab, individually, we told them that each session would be run with two persons, a speaker and a listener. The speaker, seated in one room, would have to speak for about 10 minutes about some life event, and the listener, seated in a separate room (but connected to the first one by intercom), would have to listen, and punish the speaker (by pressing a button which allegedly delivered a white noise in the speaker's headphone) for each use of a so-called stop word (e.g. uh, eh, ah). The reason, we said, was to see how this would affect the speaker's use of these words. In the control condition, the subject was simply assigned the role of listener and the experiment began (the alleged speaker was actually a prerecorded speech, with a standardized number of stop words). In the experimental condition, the experimenter, after having explained the general purpose of the experiment, suddenly announced that the role of listener was usually played by an assistant, who unfortunately was sick that day, so that it would be convenient if the subject was willing to take over that role and thus help the experimenter in the manipulation of the next subject (it should be clear to the reader that this is the typical cover-story to induce verbal role-playing in the classic experiments on role-playing). All experimental subjects who were invited in this way gladly accepted our invitation, and thus performed exactly the same task as the control subjects, but believing that they were helping the experimenter in the manipulation of the next subject. The results of this first experiment were very clear: The control subjects rated the experimental task afterwards somewhat positive, namely 2.5 (on a scale from 1 to 4), but the experimental subjects rated it 3.3, or significantly more positive. In several other experiments of the same kind (but with different concrete procedures), we generally found the same kind of effect, namely more positive (or less negative) attitudes toward the experimental task when the subjects believed to have helped the experimenter in the manipulation of the next subject, than when they believed to only have performed the task as a subject (e.g. Bruin & Rijsman, 1993; Rijsman & Bruin, 1994).

BACK TO THE PARADIGM OF VERBAL ROLE-PLAYING,BUT NOW IN EXPLICIT COMBINATION WITH STRUCTURAL VARIATIONS

Reinforced by the results of these experiments, in which we found that only the manipulation of the structural variables without verbal role-playing could induce the same or even stronger positive evaluations of the experimental task as the ones we typically find with verbal role-playing, we then decided to return to the paradigm of verbal role-playing, but now to manipulate both content and structure, to see what the relative effect of both manipulations would be. Needless to say, given the results thus far, we expected a stronger influence of the structural manipulation than of the verbal content. What we concretely did (see Bruin, 1994), was to replicate Nuttin's 1966 positive- and negative role-playing condition (using no reward instead of low reward), and cross these conditions with two different manipulations of compliance. In one condition of compliance, we simply replicated the very classic manipulation of "assistant experimenter" (see the earlier description). In another condition, however, we invited the subject directly, namely by saying that once in a while we asked the previous subject to help us in the manipulation of the next subject (using the same pretext as in the assistant-experimenter condition, namely that we wanted to measure the effect of a one-sided representation of the task on the next subject's performance). The results of this simple 2 × 2 experiment were as follows.

Subjects in the assistant-experimenter condition rated the task afterwards about 2.0 (on a scale from 1 to 6), whereas those in the elected subject condition about 2.7, clearly higher. Most importantly, however, the positive-role subjects rated the task exactly as high as the negative-role subjects, 2.4 in both cases. Unfortunately, however, given the non-significant character of our results, we were not able to publish them in a journal.

The actual absence of a contentual effect in the classic Festinger and Carlsmith paradigm, together with a strong effect of the structural involvement of the subject, became dramatically clear to us when, a couple of years ago, we were invited to review a paper from two French colleagues, namely Joule and Girandola (1995), who wanted to demonstrate what they called a "radical dissonance interpretation" of the classic Festinger and Carlsmith paradigm (for more details on this kind of interpretation, see e.g. Beauvois & Joule, 1996). Joule and Girandola presented results which, in their mind, clearly supported such a radical dissonance interpretation, but when we looked carefully at these results, and rearranged them in a different order, a totally different picture emerged. What they actually found was this.

Subjects who, just like in the traditional control condition, only performed the experimental task, rated it on the average about –0.40, or thus neutral (the scale was exactly the same as in the original experiments, namely from –5, very unpleasant, to +5, very pleasant). When they also performed a role about it (i.e. said something about the task in a role-playing manner), positively as well as negatively, the evaluation of the task remained neutral, namely +0.55 after positive role-playing and +0.40 after negative role-playing. The reader will remember that this is virtually identical to what Nuttin also found, namely a neutral effect in all three conditions (see earlier).

However, subjects who, unlike the traditional control subjects, were given a description of the task, but were not allowed to perform it, rated the task very negative, namely about –2.00. And when this kind of subjects also played a verbal role, the verbal content of the played role became very important, namely a rating of +2.77 after positive role-playing, and a rating of –2.55 after negative role-playing. Thus, what we see is that for subjects who were not really involved in the experimental task (for they were explicitly not allowed to perform it), the pattern is exactly like the one which we always read in the literature, namely a very unpleasant task which becomes very pleasant after positive role-playing, and which, by implication, should remain very unpleasant, or even become more unpleasant, after negative role-playing. And needless to say that authors who produce this rhetorical description of the Festinger and Carlsmith paradigm in the literature are also people who, just like the non-involved subjects in Joule and Girandola's experiments, never did perform the task themselves, but only heard about it from description. And maybe that is the reason why they imagine that the task must be negative, and that the effect of verbal role-playing must be con-tentual instead of, as it really is for people who perform the task, structural.

THE PARADOX OF FREE COMPLIANCE AND ITS IMPLICATION FOR THE STRUCTURAL MEANING OF EXPERIMENTAL ROLE-PLAYING

It has always been taken for granted in the literature on experimental role-playing that the subjects who were invited by the experimenter to play a role, did in fact accept the invitation, and thus played the role. This was a necessary precondition for the publication of the experiment, for, if the subjects had refused, there would have been no role-playing, and hence no publishable results either. However, the obvious implication of that situation is that the only results of experimental role-playing which we find in the literature, must be results from subjects who had already a tendency to identify with the work of the experimenter, for otherwise the experimenter's invitation to help him or her in the execution of the experiment would not have been accepted. The other and equally obvious implication of that situation is that the explicit use of force in such a situation is not really a force (in the sense of a pressure to do something which one would otherwise not have done), but actually a symbolic elimination of the possibility to show solidarity with the experimenter (in the sense of responding positively to a request for help). In other words, experimental role-playing is, given the institutional context in which it can work, by its very definition a structural event, or a psychological association of the subject with the role and work of the experimenter, and, not surprisingly then, the attitudinal consequences of experimental role-playing bear the marks of that structural event, namely a less negative or a more positive evaluation of the experimental work after or during the association with the psychological owner of that work, namely the experimenter.

The extent to which the published experiments on role-playing are confined to institutional conditions in which the subjects have an a priori tendency to identify with the experimenter's role and work, became blatantly clear to us during an experiment in which we tried to make students, at an institute of re-education after an act of delinquency, play a role in the same sense as Festinger and Carlsmith and others did in the classic paradigm of role-playing, namely ask them to replace our sick assistant in the manipulation of the next subject. Needless to say, these students did not, unlike students at a university, decide freely to be students at that institute, and when we asked them to role-play a positive attitude toward the institute, in the same way as Festinger and Carlsmith asked their students to play a positive role about the experimental task, they all bluntly refused, and thus the experiment was never performed, and obviously the results—which results in this case?—were not published (Rijsman, 1983c). However, despite the absence of any results in the classic sense of the word, we got a very significant message, namely that experiments on role-playing only succeed in institutional contexts in which the subjects are prepared to associate themselves with the role and work of the experimenter, for otherwise a request for help or assistance, or thus a structural shift in the direction of the experimenter's ownership of the work, simply does not work. Therefore, experimental role-playing is essentially a continuation of the institutional choice which was made before the experiment even started.

CONCLUSION

The results and reinterpretations of the cited experiments on role-playing obviously contain some important messages for leadership and the psychological meaning of work in general. The first and most obvious message is the one with which we ended in the prior paragraph, namely that a person's (i.e. subject's) willingness to accept a leader's (i.e. experimenter's) request to collaborate in the execution of the institutionally defined work (i.e. the experiment), is actually a continuation of the person's a priori choice to belong to that institute. This is very similar to the definition of "legitimate power", or power which derives from the partner's choice of a relationship, with rights and duties on both sides (Raven, 1965). However, although the motivational reasons to choose a relationship may vary, it seems that reasons in the domain of coercion have specific implications for the person's willingness to expand the legitimacy in the course of the interaction, for persons who were coerced to interact with the leader (i.e. experimenter) did not show any willingness to volunteer, and take his or her side when being asked for it. This reminds us very much of Rousseau's analysis of the emergence and flexibility of what she calls a "psychological contract", which, she claims, depends essentially on the person's freedom to join the interaction (Rousseau, 1995). The fact is that, in experiments on role-playing, we only deal with subjects who have chosen to join the interaction, such as students at a university, and certainly students who, like in the original Festinger and Carlsmith experiment, have paid huge amounts of money and have passed severe entrance-tests to be accepted as students at that university (in this case, Stanford University). It would be rather strange indeed, if these students were not pleased to be allowed to collaborate with their professors or graduate colleagues, and thus become insiders in the kind of work to which they actually aspire themselves. The explicit denial of showing solidarity with the experimenter in that kind of context would probably be a frustration, rather than a force, and therefore, as we said already in the previous paragraph, forced compliance in an institutional context in which experimental role-playing does work, cannot really be regarded as a force (or a pressure to do what one would not have done otherwise), but rather as a symbolic elimination of the possibility to demonstrate co-ownership of the importance of the work that needs to be done. It is important to note in this regard that Joule and Girandola also ran a condition (not mentioned previously), in which they explicitly "forced" their subjects to perform the experimental task, namely by telling them that they absolutely had no choice to retract, and that these explicitly "forced" subjects, just like the ones who were explicitly denied the possibility to actually perform the task, evaluated the task as very unpleasant. This "forced" condition was obviously a denial of the possibility to show solidarity with the experimenter, for those who "were" invited to perform the task, all accepted, and, as said before, immediately evaluated the task as neutral.

The very essence of the results we have reviewed is that within that a priori context of voluntarism, or a socially defined reality of possibilities to join the structural identity of the leader (i.e. experimenter), the meaning of work (i.e. the evaluation of the experimental task) is actually determined by the amount of symbolic association which the leader offers. Indeed, only defining the work as a voluntary participation with the leader's (i.e. experimenter's) occupation, was sufficient to enhance the worker's (i.e. subject's) evaluation of the work. And it is exactly that kind of association which the leader (i.e. experimenter) also offers, when he or she invites the worker (i.e. subject) to play a positive or a negative verbal role, and which, as we have seen, leads to exactly the same enhanced evaluation of the work in both cases.

Given these reflections, we may also look again now at the possible influence of financial rewards. In the classic contentual approach to role-playing, financial rewards are only moderators of the assumed contentual effect of verbal role-playing (e.g. a reducer of dissonance, a reinforcer for learning, an arousing factor, see Elms, 1969; Nuttin, 1974). However, in a structural approach they may act as symbolic definitions of the partisanship or identification with the role of the leader (i.e. experimenter). For example, in a context in which the person is actually very happy with the possibility to show solidarity with the experimenter, forcing the person to accept high official rewards may rather mean a frustration, or thus become a coercion rather than a reward. It is important to note in this regard that the experimental subjects in Nuttin's replication of Festinger and Carlsmith (see earlier), generally showed embarrassment with their high reward and actually preferred not to receive it; they had to be pushed to accept it (I know by experience, because I served as experimenter in that replication). However, when the same reward is offered as a gift instead of as an official reward, the symbolic meaning of partisanship with the one who pays is entirely different. This does not need to be explained, because it is very much part of our everyday life experience. For example, we would never pay a senior colleague who volunteers to help us in the performance of an experiment as we pay a student-assistant, for that would imply blame for his or her obvious solidarity with our concern. But we may offer a gift, as a symbol of our gratitude. Thus, it is not the amount of money as such which defines the reward, but what it means in the structural relationship of solidarity within the a priori context of the organization. It would be very interesting, therefore, to see what happens with high rewards that are offered as a gift of gratitude, rather than as (unwanted) official rewards in role-playing. The latter might eliminate the upward evaluation of the work (as in fact Festinger and Carlsmith observed in their high reward condition, not discussed in this article), whereas the former might simply reinforce it (for more details on this speculation, see Rijsman, 1983b).

Why then has the literature on role-playing always created the impression that the work that needed to be done was very unpleasant and that its subsequent meaning would depend on what the subject tells about it? (whereas in fact it was not judged unpleasant, and was not affected by what the subject tells about it in role-playing). As we said, the answer to that question seems to lay in the fact that those who write about this work, in articles and in textbooks, looked at it from the outside, not as psychological owners of what they talked about. From such a perspective, work that is stereotypically dull is mentally reproduced in terms of that stereotype, and thus as dull. These non-owners or outsiders are also the ones (and the only ones in the literature!) who follow "verbatim" the verbal content of what they role-play about the task, as if the scriptorial information which they produced themselves during role-playing becomes the new dominant stereotype about what they can say about the work. However, and as we have amply explained, this kind of evaluation disappears for owners of the task, and it is no longer the verbal content of the role, plus the physical character of what they do, that is the dominant determinant of their evaluation, but their structural position in the organizational context of the work.

Needless to say, this is very important for studies about the meaning of work, for people who think of work as boring, unpleasant, etc., or in short "negative" from the outside, may start to love it when somehow they become owners of that work by having a chance to collaborate with leaders in the system of meaning to which they belong, namely their organization. Researchers or consultants who approach an organization from the outside, and who think that the work really needs improvement (because it is boring, unpleasant, etc.), would do well to check this with the workers directly (and in such a condition that the workers have a chance to present themselves as psychological owners of what they do, for if they are treated as outsiders, then they may produce what the researcher expects, namely something bad instead of, as for owners, something good).

REFERENCES

Beauvois, J.-L., & Joule, R.V. (1996). *A radical dissonance theory: Old look and new paradigms.* European Monographs Series. UK: Harvester Wheatsheaf.

Bruin, R.H. (1994). *Manipulating more than we intend: An investigation of Festinger and Carlsmith's (1959) experimental procedure.* Doctoral dissertation. Tilburg University, The Netherlands.

Bruin, R.H., & Rijsman, J.B. (1993). La variable positionelle dans la situation de role-playing contre-attitudinel. In J.-L. Beauvois, R.V. Joule, & J.M. Monteil (Eds.), *Perspectives cognitives et conduites sociales IV: Jugements sociaux et changement des attitudes.* Neuchâtel, Switzerland: Delachaux et Niestlé.

Elms, A.C. (1969). *Role-playing, reward and attitude change.* New York: Van Nostrand Reinhold.

Festinger, L., & Carlsmith, J.M. (1959). Cognitive consequences of forced compliance. *Journal of Abnormal and Social Psychology*, *58*, 203–210.

Joule, R., & Girandola, F. (1995). *Le paradigme de la double soumission forcée: Un nouveau regard sur l'expérience princeps de Festinger et Carlsmith (1959)*. Paper submitted for review to J. Rijsman.

Nuttin, J.M. (1966). Attitude change after rewarded dissonant and consonant "forced compliance". *International Journal of Psychology*, *1*, 39–57.

Nuttin, J.M. (1974). *The illusion of attitude change: Towards a response contagion theory of persuasion*. London: Academic Press/Leuven University Press.

Poiesz, T. (1977). *The role of arousal in the response contagion interpretation of attitude change phenomena: Speculations and empirical data*. Master's thesis. Tilburg University, The Netherlands.

Raven, B. (1965). Social influence and power. In I.D. Steiner & M. Fishbein (Eds.), *Current studies in social psychology* (pp. 371–82). New York: Holt Rinehart & Winston.

Rijsman, J. (1970). *Sociale Hierarchisatie en Competitie*. Doctoral dissertation. Catholic University of Leuven and Louvain-la-Neuve, Belgium.

Rijsman, J. (1974). Factors in social comparison of performance influencing actual performance. *European Journal of Social Psychology*, *4*(3), 279–311.

Rijsman, J. (1983a). The dynamics of social competition in personal and categorical comparison-situations. In W. Doise & S. Moscovici (Eds.), *Current issues in European social psychology*, *Vol. 1*. Maison des Sciences de l'Homme/Cambridge University Press.

Rijsman, J. (1983b). Legitieme macht [Legitimate power]. In P. Veen & H. Wilke (Eds.), *Zicht op macht* [A view on power] (pp. 33–45). Assen, The Netherlands: Van Gorcum.

Rijsman, J. (1983c). *Role-playing and attitude change: A structural reinterpretation*. Paper presented at the East-West conference, Varna, Bulgaria.

Rijsman, J., & Bruin, R. (1994). Experimenter-subject interaction: The influence of a request for assistance on subject's attitudes. *International Journal of Psychology*, *29*(4), 453–469.

Rousseau, D.M. (1995). *Psychological contracts in organizations*. London: Sage Publications.

Verhaeghe, H. (1976). Mistreating other persons through simple discrepant role-playing: Dissonance arousal or response contagion. *Journal of Personality and Social Psychology*, *34*(1), 125–137.

Leadership in Strategic Business Unit Management

Leopold Vansina

Professional Development Institute. Catholic University of Leuven and Louvain-la-Neuve, Belgium

The action research study focuses on the ways a successful general manager engages in a process of large organizational change of a business unit. The unit itself had undergone an overhaul earlier as part of a corporate-wide organizational change project to decentralize power to its business units. The study is limited to that particular phase in which three levels of management take part in a search conference in order to develop a broad basis of involvement. The major observations and psychodynamic processes are subsequently discussed in relation to an older study of successful general managers and to the changed relations between leaders and followers after intensive restructuring.

INTRODUCTION

The purpose of this study is to observe and explore the ways in which a successful general manager sets up and engages in a process of large organizational change of his business unit. In particular, I am interested to find out to what extent the particular characteristics of successful general managers, identified in an earlier study, surface again. The study is based on an action research approach in one business unit of a medium-sized international corporation in the chemical sector. The corporation has gone through a process of delayering, outsourcing, and downsizing in a corporate-wide project to decentralise power to the respective business units. This corporate change project lasted several years. It had been successfully concluded in a period when business was booming. Consequently, there had been little or no awareness for another restructuring amongst middle managers and employees. However, an intensive labour-cost saving programme was started but it was never completely implemented. As a consequence, people lost trust in management and a sense of direction. The article focuses only on that part of a strategic management project in which the

---

Requests for reprints should be addressed to L. Vansina, Professional Development Inst., Catholic University of Leuven and Louvain-la-Neuve, 161 Oude Baan, B-3360 Korbeek-lo, Belgium; email: leopold.vansina@skynet.be

general manager engages in a search conference with his management team and the next level of managers.

Action research is defined as an approach in which the client system and the social scientist consultant engage together in problem-definition, problem-solving, and action generation to improve the functioning of their own organization in a sustainable way. This definition differs somewhat from what Eden and Huxham understand by the notion of action research. They use (1996, p. 526) the term to "embody research which, broadly, results from an involvement by the researcher with members of an organisation over a matter which is of genuine concern to them and in which there is an intent by the organisational members to take action based on the intervention". Two differences should however be noted. First, I put an emphasis on achieving a sustainable improvement of the system. Two, the involvement of the consultant with the organizational members appears to be more intense. The social scientist consultant is committed too to make the system function at a higher level. Obviously, there remains also a difference in role and decision-making power. The formal hierarchy was firmly established. Like the other organizational members, the consultant contributed to the decision-making process from his respective domain of knowledge and information, but the general manager remained in charge of the overall process.

The project started in the usual way, with an invitation to discuss with the general manager and the personnel director, the general manager's plans to move the business unit to a higher level of performance, by regaining the involvement of people, and by redirecting the efforts to achieve positive objectives. During the corporate change project the business unit had been reorganized so that it could easily be sold off. Understandably, people felt low and cost savings were never far out of their mind. The general manager was transferred from another unit abroad, which he had successfully transformed. He clearly saw potential in the people and the business and wanted to develop a broad base of consensus for a new business strategy. During the initial discussion, I noted that the general manager showed several characteristics of the successful general managers I had studied before. The organizational situation, however, was quite different from my original study. The company was not in the business of consumer products but of industrial products. The people still had the radical reorganization in mind, with all its painful consequences. Yet my interest in taking the assignment grew, giving particular attention to the way the general manager, in this quite different setting and at quite different times, set out to change this business unit.

My role can best be described as a social scientist consultant to the business unit to assist management in the development of a strategic programme. Programme is a better word than plan because the project not only includes the conception of a mission, a strategy to realize it, but also its embedding in the total business unit. In this project, I carry in fact two roles. First, as a consultant, I am asked to assist the general manager and his team to develop and implement a strategic programme; to help them in handling the group and psycho-dynamic processes through a better understanding of what is happening between the business unit leader, the management team, and the subsequent level when working on a shared task, e.g. developing and implementing a strategic programme. Second, as an action researcher, I take notes of my observations and interventions, during and after each meeting. Most of my observations are shared with the persons or groups concerned as part of the action research project. Only those observations judged not to advance the process are withheld from them.

In the first part, I will briefly summarize the research findings of my original study (Vansina, 1988). In this way the reader can explore the extent to which this particular general manager behaved in similar ways, without ever having read that study, and despite the obvious contextual differences. In the second part, I review and comment on the processes that the leader initiated or triggered off during three periods: the intake and preparation of the workshop, the search conference itself, and the first management meeting after the workshop. During this period, the social scientist consultant becomes a part in the process of interactions between the general manager and his colleagues. In the third part, I will discuss my observations in relation to the literature on leadership nowadays, summarize my findings, and draw some conclusions relevant for theory-building on leadership.

THE ORIGINAL STUDY

In the early 1980s I undertook, within a large multinational organization, a research project to identify the particular ways of thinking and behaving of successful general managers. In this consumer business, a successful business unit manager was defined by headquarters on the basis of two criteria. First, managers should have succeeded twice, and in a row, to turn their business unit around from loss-making into a profitable business, or to increase the profitability of an already profitable business. Second, they should have realized these performances in two different socio-political and cultural environments. Eventually, eight general managers were identified who met these two stringent criteria. The countries in which they had achieved these excellent results were spread out over Africa, America, Asia, and Europe. Six different nationalities were represented amongst the eight selected successful general managers. The findings were handed over to the sponsor, in a confidential report on 1st July, 1982. Later, when the confidentiality clause was removed, the research project was published (Vansina, 1988).

The findings can be briefly summarised as follows: Successful general managers have an open-systems framework, and a holistic approach to organizations, which they want to "get to know" to move them towards success. Successful general managers focus action, search commitment, and establish progress follow-ups. Eight shared features that typified their management behaviour were identified. First, these successful general managers manage with care the different interfaces of their companies: headquarters, the business, and the sociopolitical environments. Second, successful managers direct their efforts towards the "embodiment of purpose" within the whole company. Third, these managers manage the whole company, not just their boards. Fourth, they shape or strengthen the identity of their respective companies. Fifth, these managers are part of the system: They operate from within. Sixth, successful general managers build on the company's foundations with simple means. Seventh, these managers exert personal leadership. Eighth, successful general managers work through people for whom they care. All of the successful general managers, when they still qualified in terms of age, were eventually promoted to the board.

A few years later, Bennis and Nanus (1985), and Tichy and Devanna (1986) published their studies covering a wide range of different managers from various organizations. Despite the differences in economic, political, and cultural origin of the managers studied and in the internal and external organizational context, the findings are strikingly similar. Although the wording and the concepts differ they describe the same behaviour patterns.

The leadership I focus on, in the original and the current study, corresponds with managers in stratum five of Jaques' seven systemic, hierarchical levels (Jaques, 1976; Jaques & Cason, 1994). At this level, the manager is confronted with the task to position and to manage a whole system within a bounded environment. It implies the creation or discovery of objectives (what the organization could and should be) five to ten years into the future, and the organization of activities to achieve them (a strategy). While Jaques (almost) exclusively deals with the cognitive capabilities of these general managers of business units, I do include other aspects of leadership as well. More specifically, I was and I am interested in the unfolding processes of general managers' involvement when perceiving the need for a transformational change of their business units.

The original research was largely done, in retrospect through in-depth interviews, covering about eight years of the manager's life. That period could be typified as turbulent, but the markets were still likely to grow, however, not as much as had been anticipated. Consequently, some managers had started with "zero-budgeting", "greenfields", or other approaches, to question and redesign the luxurious organizational structures. Radical organizational change, which we have come to know in the 1990s, was largely absent. The leader, i.e. general manager, was still perceived as the one who led his business unit to serve their product markets better than the competition.

THE TRANSFORMATION

The Intake and Preparation of the Workshop

At the suggestion of the personnel director, who had seen me working as a consultant to a staff department in the same international chemical corporation, the general manager of the business unit—which from now on I will call XO— invited me for a discussion. During this first encounter, he described the situation his business unit was in, while sizing up one another to find out whether we could work together. The general manager told me with enthusiasm that he had been appointed to XO more than a year ago. He had reached the conclusion that it was time to change its strategic position. Four years ago, XO had been prepared by a renowned outside consulting firm to be sold off. It was not seen as belonging to the core business of the corporation, and its performance was considered as unsatisfactory. He had now sufficient data about its profitability and its opportunities in the world market to rethink this prevailing strategy. Furthermore, some of the originally listed constraints could be seen and taken as competitive advantages, for example, its high safety and ecological standards. He had convinced headquarters and received permission to start a new strategic round before the current strategic plan came to an end. There was a new management team, with young ambitious managers with whom he had sporadically discussed some of his ideas which he had developed from talks with customers and from his visits to different markets, some of them in Asia. He wanted his managers too to become involved in the exercise and the business. This would be the first time in the history of the business unit that such a broad level of managers would be brought together for a strategic round. In the discussion it became clear that we had to think about two different strategic rounds. A first round would include his management team as well as the next level of management. Together, they would try to picture what XO could be, formulate a mission statement, as well as some ways to realize it. A second round needed to be set up with the corporate staff in order to gain credibility and legitimization in headquarters and in which some of the creative ideas would be tested on their feasibility. The first round looked like a transformational approach as described by Tichy and Devanna (1986), Bennis and Nanus (1985), and myself (Vansina, 1982, 1988). The second round would follow a more systematic, quantitative, business-school-like approach, involving only the management team, to appreciate the risks and to gain political leverage.

Upon my request the personnel manager started to describe the climate in XO. The employees felt they were the underdog within the international corporation. The business unit had been for sale for more than four years. They did not like the idea of being sold off; yet, the fact that no one was interested in buying them was equally discouraging. Furthermore, the production process required continuous attention to safety, and their attractiveness from neighbouring business units was low. The previous restructuring had left some wounds, which had not yet healed, although the coming of the general manager and recent capital investments had raised morale and expectations.

Based on this information, I started to explore with them some possible approaches to develop a strategic programme, which would involve a large group of managers and pay attention to some possible concerns of the people. Namely, taking advantage of the emerging business opportunities might entail the building of a new production facility abroad and might be considered as a preparation to abandon the local production site. Apart from the increased status and security of becoming a full-fledged business unit, not all managers would see this as a challenging assignment on the horizon. The trust being gained should not be lost.

The meeting ended with an agreement that I would put a programme design on paper and send it to them as a basis for a subsequent discussion. In the meantime, I would have some individual interviews with the other members of the management team, the production and the engineering manager, to explore their views on the situation. They would send me the documents pertaining to the last strategic plan. I left the meeting with a good feeling about the leadership capabilities of the general manager. He and the personnel director seemed to be on the same level although they brought in some complementary information.

The individual interviews reflected the earlier description of the current situation pretty well. However, one member held a widely different view on how to go about the development of a strategic plan. He wanted the plan to be the product of a quantitative approach, as did the corporate staff, and to reserve this task for a small group of managers who would intensively work on it for at least four months. He seemed to communicate that he was in charge of that task and at the same time concerned about the wild ideas that were floating around. His views reflected largely the old strategic analysis, which had given top priority to comparative costs in the commodity business. He supported his point of view by showing me a deliberately skewed diagram of the comparative costs of XO against its competitors.

After the interviews, I sat down with the general manager and the two less senior members of his team to discuss my proposal and finalize the conference design. The information obtained from the interviews was put up front on the agenda because it called for a radical reconsideration of my proposal. Nobody seemed to be surprised. The member's views and stance were known, but for one reason or another no one had tried to make him change his position. Maybe, the general manager was satisfied with the current situation that three out of his four team members were in favour of a more entrepreneurial and involving approach to strategic management. Eventually, it was decided to go ahead with the suggested two-day residential workshop and to take the critical questions from the discussions to the second strategic round. "We have to show headquarters that the conclusions are also supported by data from their own standard strategic analysis", the general manager concluded.

In order to embed the strategic thinking in the organization, the workshop would start with a search conference (Emery & Purser, 1996), followed by a stakeholder analysis (Ackoff, 1981), and end with the formulation of the key ingredients of a mission statement. The membership of the workshop would be divided in small groups to answer key questions to be subsequently discussed in plenum. This would allow for maximum involvement and at the same time reveal some of the dynamics of the organization. The general manager felt confident with the design to reveal and discuss all information and positions within a wider organizational setting in order to engage and develop a broad base of commitment to the business unit's mission.

What have I observed that typifies the leader so far? First, the general manager is aware that there is a gap between senior management and the shopfloor that needs to be bridged by more engaging relations. More people need to be brought on board. This is congruent with my earlier research findings that: *Successful general managers manage the whole company, not just their boards or management teams.* Second, two strategic rounds are planned. One to engage a wide group of people in building a broad platform for what the business unit wants to be. And a second round to make the strategic programme acceptable at corporate level. *Successful general managers manage with care the different interfaces: headquarters, the business, and the sociopolitical environment.* Third, the general manager is bringing in enthusiasm and a new way of looking at constraints and opportunities. He refuses to manage a graveyard, a unit to be sold off. In his mind, a living organization must have positive, attractive objectives, which challenge the membership. *Successful general managers direct their efforts towards "the embodiment of purpose".* "It [the purpose] is appreciated as 'realistic' and 'achievable' but set as 'challenging', thereby reflecting their competitive spirit while igniting the energy of management and employees" (Vansina, 1988, p. 139).

Besides these three, earlier identified characteristics of successful general managers, I noted my alertness to avoid stirring up unjustified suspicion. Furthermore, I struggled to sort out whether the different stance of one team member was simply a personal matter, or if this person presented an aspect of the organization that was split off from the conscious experience of the other members, namely, an anxiety for corporate staff and top management that made them shy away from risk taking.

The Workshop: A Search Conference

Fourteen managers took part in this workshop. They sat down around the free-standing tables, arranged in half a circle, facing a couple of flipcharts and a screen for the overhead projector. The general manager opened the workshop by stating that time had come to rethink "where we are and where we want to be as a business". The 14 managers listened, awaiting things to come. As I stood up to clarify my role and the design of the workshop, the general manager seated himself with the other managers at one of the tables.

The purpose of the search conference was to come to a deep appreciation of the present situation before looking into the future. To answer the first question: "what is it like to manage here?", the group was divided in three small parties: the management team, the managers of the primary process, and the support staff. Their answers, processed in plenary, revealed the differences in work experiences. The management team saw the situation as a set of obligations, not opportunities. Support services took pride in the safety regulations and records of the plant. While the primary process managers struggled with the employees' feelings of being the underdog of the corporation. Without too much debate, a shared general understanding emerged, as well as an appreciation of the various perspectives. From that point on, the group was divided into two mixed groups to deal with the subsequent questions.

Interesting dynamics surfaced when discussing the question: "Is there a good fit between the present organization and the external environment?" The subgroup with the general manager became very active. The energy floated from the general manager towards the other managers and back, reinforcing the position that a fit was lacking. The more "conservative" member, who had voiced his concerns about risk taking, chaired the other subgroup. Only suggestions to improve the current system were listed. A subdued mood dominated the thinking, even to the point that the production manager's question to redefine the boundaries of the business unit was quietly dropped.

Neither of these two "leading" persons presented the group report in plenary. The first subgroup bluntly stated, "there is a misfit between the ambitions and competences of our people and the external environment". In other words, there was a felt need for change! The enthusiasm of the group did not subside with the more conservative report. When the obvious differences were denied in plenary, I drew the attention to the fact that the first group concluded that there was a need for major change, while the second group only considered suggestions for fine-tuning. And I added, "even a suggestion to redefine the boundaries of XO to include some other profitable products, made from one of their basic chemicals, did not get in the final report". The manager who chaired that subgroup responded that "such a change is not realistic in view of the established separation of commodities and specialities in the recent business unit structure". The general manager listened and waited without a word, as if he wanted the others to appreciate the different positions within the management team. I questioned whether the current boundaries were not drawn as a function of the idea to sell off XO and keep the more profitable products within another business unit. The general manager nodded (in agreement?).

During these exchanges, I had a strong feeling that the total group was watching the moves of the general manager with attention. A lot of questions flashed through my mind. Was he going to oppose one of his managers, or simply allow others to register the differences in viewpoint? Or did he expect me or someone else to expose these dynamics? Or did he refrain from making a correcting remark because it might close off the free-floating exchange of information, feelings, and opinions, even those expressing anxiety, and immobility through risk avoidance? Did his silence signal others to remain silent too? Or did they remain silent because they were in agreement with the critical ideas expressed? Was this a sign of "calculated sincerity" or the adherence to a cultural norm that confronting one another in public was not to be done? You state your views openly but you don't confront. One thing was certain: The critical comments affected the subgroup, while in the plenary discussions it did not to the same extent.

More important than what went on in my mind was the calm posture of the general manager, who, like the rest of the group, seemed to be attentive in following the discussions, recognizing certain statements and reactions, and learning from the total process. He refrained from correcting views that deviated from his, or from arguing his position. He just allowed all information, opinions, anxieties, and legitimate, negative feelings to be expressed, including my comments; he allowed the collective dynamics to emerge as another kind of occasion from which to learn. As such, a kind of learning community was being developed with members holding different positions in relation to the psychological centre. By the latter I refer to a sensed centrality of carrying the business unit forward. These different positions did not, however, correspond with the established hierarchy.

Exploring the developments in the environment within the next five to ten years revealed similar dynamics. This time a younger director took the chair in the subgroup and listed the key ideas on the flipchart. The plenary meeting appeared to have had some positive impact on the "conservative" member, at least temporarily. He joined in the discussion with an observation of a positive external development. Namely, that the end product made from their basic chemicals seemed to be moving from the lower end to the higher market segment. From that point onwards, however, all contributions were pointing towards the difficulties ahead. Foremost, he believed that the prices would go up for at least one basic chemical, for labour costs, and for transportation. These increased costs could not be absorbed by the customers, although the available substitutes for making the end product were markedly more expensive and not likely to come down in price. Another major area of uncertainty was what the American competitor was going to do in the European market. The report again had put the emphasis on the external uncertainties and risks.

The general manager's subgroup came up with a moderately positive report. The growth market was developing in Asia, whereas the European market would most likely remain stable. More attention should be given to the market opportunities for one of their by-products. This report focused on the business opportunities, while remaining realistic. Again one of the younger managers was encouraged to present the report. The entailing discussion generated seemingly less energy. Again questions popped up in my mind: Was the group tired after a long day of work? Or was the group trying to control their aggression against one member who had repeated his concern that such a discussion should be reserved for the more systematic strategic round to be organized with corporate assistance (thereby reducing the relevance of this workshop and accentuating the irrelevance of a number of people present)? I decided to wait with any comment thinking that, in general, an analysis of macro-economic developments confronts any normal group of managers with their limited influence. Critical, however, is the reaction of the leader towards these areas of uncertainty. The general manager remained calm and apparently contained the uncertainties, accepting the diverse views on the future as a matter of fact. Moving two critical questions to the strategic round with the corporate staff closed the discussion. One, could the likely cost increases be absorbed by the customers? Two, what could be done to counter the possible dumping practices from the American competitors? In this way everyone's contributions were recognized as valuable without foreclosing further explorations.

The next morning, in view of the limited time, I started the meeting with a summary of the critical issues we had discussed the day before. A discussion followed in which everyone joined in with enthusiasm. When the same member came in with "perhaps we will not make any of our products anymore in the future ..." and continued to raise negative fantasies, I intervened. Directing myself towards him, I said: "I think I have something to tell you. If you too consistently take the role of the devil's advocate, people may stop listening to you because it breaks their enthusiasm, and you won't get the hearing that you might deserve. It looks to me as if you feel you have to bring in a sense of reality, as if without you the group would go wild!" He protested somewhat, saying that he did not understand. When I repeated myself in order to clarify my observation, he still pretended not to understand. At that point, I told him that he and I could discuss it further during the coffee break. The general manager listened carefully. This was the first time that I "confronted" an individual member. A younger manager tried to proceed with the agenda, as if nothing had happened, but the energy was gone. The group was flat. The member concerned remained obviously out of the discussion. I became concerned too. I stated this and called for a break during which I could have a talk with that person. It had become clear to me that I had broken a norm. Members were allowed to learn in public, but no one should be confronted directly and openly.

While I had a talk with that person and another member who voluntarily joined, the general manager stayed behind with the other participants in the workshop. When I returned to the conference room, the general manager told me: "I think you have done the right thing!" This was an important comment that could be understood from at least two different perspectives. First, he wanted me to feel free to come out with whatever observations I had; thereby, he also kept this communication channel open. And second, he too had noticed that the group went into an as-if mode: pretending to continue with the task, while their mind was somewhere else. So it was right to recognize this reality, and to break the meeting for some clarification and maintenance work.

The membership was now able to continue with a classic stakeholders' analysis, which provided another set of constraints within which one could picture the business unit XO. The two subgroups went back to their rooms, first, to make a stakeholders' analysis, and second, to vision the business unit against all the compiled background information. The visioning task was to formulate some key elements that should be included in the mission statement. This appeared to be difficult for both groups.

The general manager's group came up with a list of requirements the business unit had to meet to create and maintain mutual satisfactory relations with the key stakeholders. The other subgroup spent most of the allotted time on venturing ideas about what they wished the business unit to be. This led to some remarks: "We are not like that yet!". Making a distinction between "what we are" and "what we want to be", proved to be extremely difficult for some members. Eventually, the group took from the various ideas key words that appealed to them for inclusion in the mission statement. At the last minute they added: "care for others".

During the presentation of the reports, someone argued to include "low cost producer" in the mission as another key desirable feature, since "our costs are too high because of our continued investment in safety". To which the general manager promptly replied that he did not want to be the general manager of a company that was not safe, nor ecologically sound. This was the first time that he took a firm position. It was not just a personal view; it was something important he stands for. Safety and ecology is beyond negotiation. The group accepted it with a kind of relief. Note that most of the members work in that factory.

Comparing the two reports, the members emphasized the similarities between both. Consensus was reached about a final combined list of nine items. The members were then invited to weight these items in terms of their relative importance. The general manager was the first to give his priorities: safety, key player (in the market and consequently in the corporation), and care for others. When everyone had set his or her priorities, the list was checked and compared with the previous reports, which were still displayed on the walls. The group felt tired but satisfied. The diversity in perspectives had largely been integrated. Some critical comments were left to be checked on their relative reality-value in the second strategic round. If this is what the group wants XO to be, if it is desirable, then there is a good chance that we can make it happen. The strategy by which the group will make it happen, needs to be further explored and checked on its feasibility.

The management team was asked to take the list of items and to formulate a mission statement that subsequently would be checked, first with the other managers of the workshop and then with the people further down in the organization. Corrections and amendments would still be possible.

What can be observed in this two-day workshop? First of all the leader seated himself amidst the other managers. He was one of them, willing to learn with them from the discussions and the emerging dynamics. As with in my earlier study, one can see that: "successful general managers are part of the system: they operate from within". But the setting allowed me to observe another important feature. The leader was there, not to impose his views and wisdom on to the others, nor to present his views as the one that count. No, on the contrary he refrained from arguing, putting one view against another, to enable everyone, including me, to express his or her views, understanding, and concerns. Everyone was encouraged to be there to speak his or her mind, and to be listened to. This is what Kahn (1992) has called "psychological presence". The ability to be there, without distraction, in a setting which is safe and where the work elements of tasks, roles, and interactions are meaningful. Miller adds to this: "safety to use one's authority to speak out, knowing that one will be heard" (1998, p. 17). Avoiding argumentation, to put one view against another, did not mean that the leader did not join in exploring what makes sense. It does mean that in argumentation, "winning" most often gains importance over finding out. In this kind of argumentation power of one sort or another takes over from reasoning. It easily leads to a power differentiation that does not foster learning in public, in the temporary, organizational community. Moving an argument to the second round, where more information will be collected and mathematically processed, illustrates this intent to let the data speak for itself. Being wholly there, to share, compare and find out with the other members, is inevitably linked to trust in the members' capacity to make sense of the data and to overcome painful experiences from earlier periods. Being there undisturbed was a key element in establishing engaging relations.

The leader helped to create a genuine learning community in which positional power is kept out to allow role and personal perspectives to come forward and speak for themselves. On two occasions, the leader stepped forward. First, to take an irrevocable stance towards safety and ecology. Thereby expressing in a direct way *his care for people*. Second, to state his priorities about what the key elements are in what the company has to be: "safety, a key player, and care for others". Maybe there were more occasions in which he took personal stands; I only take these two to draw the attention to the visibility of the person of the leader. *Successful general managers exert personal leadership*. The individual person is there, not one kind of a constructed model.

The general manager was able to contain the uncertainties, anxieties, and hopes of the members related to the future of the organization. He did not jump to conclusions, to grandiose plans, nor did he side with one stance against another. This capacity to contain within oneself the ambivalence, anxieties, and hopes of

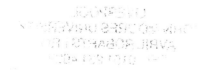

the membership helps not only to create a safe environment, but also encourages others to go on with the work.

The Management Meeting

The general manager and one other member had just returned from abroad and were brought back into the picture. The group members briefly reviewed the reactions and second thoughts about the workshop. The managers on the production site were very pleased with the work done and had high hopes for the next steps in the programme. The same enthusiasm was present in the circle of the management team but they felt that my confrontation had been misplaced. As the urgent, unanticipated matter came up, the general manager wanted a break to settle this issue first so that his mind was cleared to focus wholly on the agenda.

From the various criteria to appreciate the quality of a good mission definition, the general manager picked up its uniqueness and its desirability. As a way to further the process, he drew a diagram on the board distinguishing respectively the internal corporate and the external environment, and the relevance of the items as qualifiers or differentiators. "Safety and environment consciousness" as well as "low cost producer" (which came up again in the discussion) could be seen as qualifiers. But the first one became also a differentiator, if one would look for a partner to do business with. "Low cost" was not a very inspiring word, since it might still be associated with the pains of the last restructuring experience. So "cost efficiency" was found to be a more appropriate concept.

Two psychodynamic processes emerged that coloured the work of the team; the first one having a direct bearing on the second. All members contributed to bringing the team together again. A conscious effort was made to show mutual recognition for the attempts made to bring the diversity of views in proper perspective. It seemed less a search for a compromise than an effort to invest more time in reality testing.

The difficulty to maintain the distinction between "what we are" and "what we want to be" and to work with the psychic tension proper to the distance between these two, was still there. It is exactly this psychic tension that one attempted to appreciate in terms of the feasibility to move from the current state towards a "willed future" through co-ordinated action. The reasoning could be typified as follows. A mission becomes feasible through its strategy. Against another position: A mission is feasible when we believe in our capacity to design an appropriate strategy to reach it. Containing this uncertainty, to appreciate it on its reality value is a critical competence. The general manager showed sufficient self-confidence to hold on to the latter reasoning.

Work was assigned to different parties or individual members. Then we broke up for the Easter holidays. The strategic programme was to be continued.

What can one learn from this meeting that is relevant for understanding the processes leaders engage in to transform their companies? First, one sees again how the leader wants to be psychologically present. Urgent matters that might distract him from the agenda must be cleared. Second, one may note the energy the leader invests in appreciating diversity and integrating it in a broader framework. Third, a framework that brings into focus the organizational characteristics on which the organization can, through co-ordinated efforts, have a meaningful impact: "safety and ecology" and, not so much, "low cost producer". The latter would be difficult to achieve without squeezing all life out of the business unit if one takes the prevailing standards of living, and the social and governmental regulations concerning safety and pollution controls as givens.

DISCUSSION

In the 1990s most organizations have gone through one or more radical restructuring exercises. This was also true for the business unit in my current study. It had undergone a radical organizational change as part of a corporate move to make the business units more entrepreneurial and responsible for profit and loss. Such vast organizational changes may drastically alter the dynamic relations between leaders and followers.

Indeed, delayering, outsourcing, and downsizing have become associated with senior management and leadership; and not necessarily with economic, unfavourable conditions. The leader is no longer seen as protecting the employees, as creating conditions so that they can do their work better, but as squeezing more out of them for the benefits of the shareholders, and/or for the interests of the leader him- or herself. Thereby, the followers' anxiety of the competitors may have become transferred to the leader (Miller, 1998). The leader may indeed become the person to be afraid of. He or she is seen as the instigator of such radical changes, or as the one who brings in the consultants to do the downsizing. Consequently, and despite the classic removal of hierarchical levels, the gap between the general manager and the shop floor may not be decreased but may in fact be increased. An emotional distance replaces the physical distance. The anxieties easily lead to suspicion and "calculated sincerity". "Compliance is a chosen, intentional response rather than a habit, and there is a good deal of overt cynicism" (Miller, 1998, p. 11). People become withdrawn psychologically, flying into fantasy and withholding personal investment in the institution. This symptom is called "failed dependency" (Miller, 1998). "Psychological withdrawal," he writes (1998, p. 12), "implies that many employees have become untamed. For some, leaders and top management have become objects of rage, for others contemptible or disregarded; and whilst some pockets of the more basic dependency remains they are getting smaller." This emotional distance or even the sheer absence of a relation between the leader and the employees seems not only necessary to carry out dramatic business- process- re-engineering projects (Vansina & Taillieu, 1996) but becomes an inevitable consequence of these kinds of management practice. They may have the work done by consultants, but they sanction—even reward—them financially the more people they can make redundant. Two factors may even aggravate the emotional distance. First, the salary differentials between the leader, i.e. the CEO, and the rest of the organization has taken such proportions that what the leader annually receives (salaries plus bonus) goes beyond the imagination of the people on the shop floor. Second, more frequently leaders don't come up from the ranks but are brought in from the outside, by the shareholders. We often observe that they don't even bother to get to know the people, nor to understand the productive processes, because they only manage directly the bottom line, namely the financial results.

"Our" company and "belonging to" are gaining different meanings. Outsourcing and subcontracting are blurring the boundaries of who belongs and who does not. "Where" I work becomes frequently disconnected from "for whom" I work. As a subcontractor, the company I work for is not the company that I work in. "My" company can as well refer to the place where I work, as to the organization I am a member of. Or as an employee, I may work in "my" company with people who don't "belong", namely subcontractors. Furthermore, the individual employee is expected to balance and optimize his or her loyalty to the company he or she works for against the interests of the client or customer. Most importantly, however, the feeling of belonging and ownership is eroded by the realization that the company wants to maintain only instrumental relations with its employees (Vansina, 1988)—employing people only as long as they have a direct added value to the corporation. When only instrumental relations dominate, no psychological ownership can grow. When, as mentioned earlier, the leader is appointed from the outside, and rewarded on the basis of his or her added value to the shareholders, he or she is likely to be experienced as "not one of us". He or she is managing the organization from the "outside" and for "outsiders".

One more factor contributes to the further erosion of belonging. Namely, the successive restructuring without any time or support to work through its painful consequences, e.g. parting from colleagues, giving up familiar work and career perspectives, the reinforced feeling that despite genuine efforts one is unable to have a determining influence over one's future. These new organizational conditions, which may be around in a given situation, do complicate the task of a general manager even further.

In this article I studied one particular episode: the search conference, its preparation, and the subsequent management meeting. However, the general manager had already done a lot of work before I was called in. He had sensed the emotional climate in the company, the ambitions of young managers, and the depressive mood of others that was lingering on after the last restructuring exercise. He felt the need for change, which he also cultivated by dropping hints about new opportunities, by showing the profit figures, as well as by his own pleasure in managing XO. In the search conference the atmosphere had been congenial. Jokes were told during the breaks, or just before getting on with the task. The general manager had repeatedly shown his respect for what had been achieved, in particular for the high safety and ecological standards. The strategic programme did not end with the search conference. Much more work was done, but covering this would take me beyond the scope of this article.

From what I have observed in that episode, I may conclude that despite the organizational changes of delayering, outsourcing, and downsizing, the pattern of eight characteristics of successful general managers is still recognizably present in the behaviour of this particular leader. Six of the eight behaviour patterns were identified within the researched period. Two were not obviously present: (1) the shaping and strengthening of the company's identity; and (2) the building on the company's foundations with simple means. What I did observe was the leader's public recognition and emphasis on the achieved safety and ecological standards, which point in the direction of the former characteristic. The strategy to be developed, and its correlative, adaptive programme to implement it, might generate more supportive evidence for the latter. So far, however, I have not seen anything that would contradict these two last characteristics.

I was able to observe closely the leader's interactions with his two different levels of managers. Observable differences in the emotional quality of the two subgroups hold our attention. The subgroup in which he was absent produced reports which showed more risk inhibition as expressed in suggested minor changes, and a greater acceptance of the existing situation as not changeable. The subgroup with the general manager came up with more challenging proposals for change and improvements. This difference leads me to assume that much reciprocal stimulation took place in that subgroup work with the general manager. This supports Burns' (1978, p. 20) observation: "Persons engage with others in such a way that leaders and followers raise one another to higher levels of motivation and morality." The first subgroup seemed to be more "influenced" by the critical comments of one of the members.

Most obvious, however, and different from the findings of the original study, was the leader's investment in creating, maintaining, and taking part in a learning community. A setting safe enough to enable, even encourage, members to be psychologically present. To share information, views, and even negative feelings, to explore their reality-value and relevance, while learning from the dynamics as they emerged and as they were commented on. In my original study (Vansina, 1988), management conferences were often used to enthuse members, to involve them in gaining ownership of the strategy or vision of the leader. Here, in contrast, the community created images of the "willed future" itself. It was the outcome of a "co-creation" process. If this observation is correct, then it would add support to the claim of other researchers, that leaders need to be increasingly capable to exert "leadership in learning" to manage organizations nowadays (Krantz, 1998; Miller, 1998). According to Krantz (1998, p. 101):

In order to create genuine learning environments people must learn in public and must expose both their experience (with all of its irrational subjectivity) and their areas of ignorance ... Providing leadership of this type of learning entails not only vulnerability on the part of the leader but also being able to publicly tolerate the frustration of not knowing and of sustaining the unknown question in the face of pressure to gain closure with quick answers.

Leadership in learning contrasts sharply with the frequently advocated "winners" programmes of decisive, "strong leaders" emphasizing only positive experiences, at the expense of having to deny the painful experiences of previous and of developing restructuring programmes. Evidence is there that such denial of legitimate negative experiences actually increases the disenchantment of employees, and reinforces psychological withdrawal (Miller, 1998). "Indeed, those companies that try hardest to eliminate negative or ambivalent feelings may instead stimulate the most resentment, mistrust and suspicion" (Miller & Stein, 1993, p. 36).

Leadership in learning implies the capacity to work from, what in clinical psychology is called, the "depressive position". Melanie Klein (1940, 1946) provides a useful frame for thinking about the impact of anxiety and ambivalence, and ways of handling it. She noticed that people could operate from two different states of mind everyone has gone through, as part of growing up. In the mind state A (the "paranoid-schizoid position"), anxieties, uncertainties, ambivalence, and fear trigger very primitive defence mechanisms leading to thought patterns and experiences of scape-goating, blame, persecution, grandiosity, and idealization. The ability to engage in interpersonal relations is seriously impaired, and concrete thinking leads to rigidity and loss of creativity (Segal, 1957). In the state of mind B (the "depressive position"), persons can experience themselves and others as whole and integrated people. They are able to experience that the same person can at times be good and bad and that a business opportunity also includes a risk. This last mode of being with others "increases the ability to integrate experiences, to think, and to collaborate meaningfully out of concern that extend beyond survival and self-protection" (Krantz, 1998, pp. 80–81). Krantz (1998, p. 81) uses Lapierre (1989) to clarify the implications of these two positions for the different ways leaders exert power:

When functioning primarily in the paranoid-schizoid mode, their exercise of power tends to be shaped by grandiose, unrealistic ideas that culminate in ineffective efforts. On the other hand, while aspirations and dreams shaped by the depressive mode of functioning may be less grand, they lead to what he calls "relative potency", as the exercise of power is more realistically connected to the external world.

Leadership in learning also means enabling others to work from that "depressive position". Facilitating others to function in the realities of work and to learn from experience can be stimulated by at least three kinds of behaviour.

First, that the leader is able to contain (Bion, 1961) the uncertainties, anxieties and aspirations of the members. Second, the leader succeeds in creating a good enough "holding environment" (Winnicott, 1991), e.g. a situation in which people feel sufficiently secure to open themselves and to explore unfamiliar or unknown ground. To be psychologically present, devoid of feelings of having to be attentive to the possible misuse that might be made of one's ideas and explorations; and of not having to be right all the time. In such a setting, also, the group as a group can become a container, so that the leader is not the only one who has to absorb and contain the tensions. Third, the leader's capacity to be congruent. Congruence (Rogers, 1961) refers to the capacity to have whole, rather than partial experiences and the ability or freedom to talk about these experiences in all their different aspects: the joy as well as the sadness of being promoted, for example. The willingness to listen to negative feelings resulting from painful experiences, even when listening might include the risk of feeling hurt. When these three conditions are realized, persons are enabled and able to face the complexities of today's organizational realities.

From this action research, I venture the conclusion that the pattern of eight behavioural characteristics of successful general managers is still valid, at least in this case, but that the way they achieve an "embodiment of purpose" is likely to be different. They cannot jump from the painful experiences of past restructuring programmes to enthusiastic commitments to new strategic objectives. This would imply the denial of legitimate, negative feelings, and encourage as-if behaviour. If these findings are not incidental than I must conclude that leaders have a great capacity to be with their people, and to be in touch with the deeper emotional life of the organization.

REFERENCES

Ackoff, R.L. (1981). *Creating the corporate future*. New York: Wiley.

Bennis, W., & Nanus, B. (1985). *Leadership: The strategies for taking charge*. New York: Harper & Row.

Bion, W. (1961). *Experiences in groups*. London: Tavistock.

Burns, J.M. (1978). *Leadership*. New York: Harper & Row.

Eden, C., & Huxham, C. (1996). Action research for the study of organisations. In S.R. Clegg, C. Hardy, & W.R. North (Eds.), *Handbook of organization studies* (pp. 526–542). London: Sage.

Emery, M., & Purser, R. (1996). *The search conference*. San Francisco: Jossey-Bass.

Jaques, E. (1976). *A general theory of bureaucracy*. London: Heinemann.

Jaques, E., & Cason, K. (1994). *Human capabilities: A study of individual potential and its application*. Virginia: Fall Church.

Kahn, W.A. (1992). To be fully there: Psychological presence at work. *Human Relations, 45*, 321–350.

Klein, M. (1940). Mourning and its relation to manic-depressive states. In *The writings of Melanie Klein: Vol. 1. Love, guilt and reparation* (pp. 344–369). London: Hogarth Press.

Klein, M. (1946). Notes on schizoid mechanisms. In *The writings of Melanie Klein: Vol. 3. Envy, gratitude and other works* (pp. 1–24). London: Hogarth Press.

Krantz, J. (1998). Anxiety and the new order. In E.B. Klein, F. Gabelnick, & P. Herr (Eds.), *The psychodynamics of leadership* (pp. 77–108). Madison, CT: Psychosocial Press.

Lapierre, L. (1989). Mourning, potency, and power in management. *Human Resource Management, 28*(2), 177–189.

Miller, E.J. (1998). The leader with the vision: Is time running out? In E.B. Klein, F. Gabelnick, & P. Herr (Eds.), *The psychodynamics of leadership* (pp. 3–26). Madison, CT: Psychosocial Press.

Miller, E.J., & Stein, M. (1993). Individual and organisation in the 1990s: Time to rethink? *The Tavistock Institute Review, 1992–1993* (pp. 35–37). London: Tavistock Institute.

Rogers, C. (1961). *On becoming a person: A therapist's view of psychotherapy.* Boston: Houghton Mifflin.

Segal, H. (1957). Notes on symbol formation. *International Journal of Psychoanalysis, 38,* 391–397.

Tichy, N., & Devanna, M.A. (1986). *Transformational leadership.* New York: Wiley.

Vansina, L.S. (1982). *Developing organisations through their top performers: Findings on how top performers think and manage.* Confidential report.

Vansina, L.S. (1988). The general manager and organisational leadership. In M. Lambrechts (Ed.), *Corporate revival: Managing into the nineties* (pp. 127–151). Leuven, Belgium: University Press.

Vansina, L.S. (1998). The individual in organisations: Rediscovered or lost forever? *European Journal of Work and Organizational Psychology, 7,* 265–282.

Vansina, L.S., & Taillieu, T. (1996). Business process re-engineering or socio-technical system design in new cloths? In R.W. Woodman & W.A. Pasmore (Eds.), *Research in organizational change and development, Vol. 9* (pp. 81–100). Greenwich, CT: JAI Press.

Winnicott, D.W. (1991). *The child, the family and the outside world.* London: Penguin Books.

The Response of the General Manager

"The General Manager", XO

A Commentary on "Leadership in Strategic Business Unit Management" by Leopold Vansina

It is my conviction that all organizational change has to be "tailor-made". From the very beginning of a change project, it is crucial to make it clear to all persons involved what the desired changes are about, who wants them, and most importantly why these changes are necessary. In a technocratic culture such as ours, desired changes are most often initiated from the top down. Their targets are by preference specified in quantitative terms (market share, costs, procedures, etc.). Striking is the fact that mostly aggregated concepts are used. Consequently, the employees remain in the dark about what is expected from them, how they can contribute to make the change effective and what the impact of all these efforts will be. It is most regretful that with few exceptions change processes are initiated to achieve these quantitative outcomes without any thought about the implied (concomitant) behavioural changes. Resistance to change, distrust, de-motivation, and poor implementation are the logical consequences.

So had it been with XO. The first project took place in the context of an overall corporate change process. The survival of the corporation as an independent entity was at stake. Consequently, corporate priorities determined from the onset the nature of the change and all key decisions. The business unit XO emerged from the exercise as a "non-core" activity, that should be sold off at the first occasion. The process of personnel cuts could honestly be described as heavy-handed and created distrust of the leadership and headquarters. The second cost-cutting project reinforced the employees' conviction that management could no longer be trusted. The irony was that in the period of this second change project the business results were at an all-time high.

Ten years ago, I had also worked for this business unit. I remember still the critical staff with high self-esteem. They were proud to operate a very dangerous plant in a professional way. In this sense the crew was the élite on the site. Only the "strongest" knew how to maintain themselves in this risky situation. Good comradeship and no-nonsense leaders characterized the unit. But how different from what I found upon my return! Distrusting employees, without much self-regard, and no confidence in management. Furthermore, there was an absolute lack of vision. A rigid budget reign was imposed because of the unit—typical for a business unit with a strategic "cash cow" status. There was discord about the possible consequences of all this on safety and the environment.

After a short period of getting to know the situation I concluded:

- The technical infrastructure of the plant was a "given". Substantial capacity expansion was no longer possible, nor profitable.
- The market for our product for the coming years was still growing, but predominantly in the Far East.
- The return of operations could still be reasonably improved.
- The know-how and experience of the employees was good to excellent.
- Safety and ecology were and are crucial for the survival of the plant.
- A lot of know-how was not used or was stored inaccessibly, certainly not at all in a form that it could be used by the operators. Knowledge was seen as the property of the "staff".
- Absence of trust in the management of the business unit.
- No or little self-esteem, and limited solidarity.
- The financial results were good. The future, however, was uncertain to bleak because of the above-mentioned points.

I tried to make it clear to all the employees that their future was in their hands. No bickering about the shareholders, all hands on deck. Of primary importance was the creation of a mission. A mission in which much attention was given to self-regard, collaboration, and initiative. "Ownership" in its various forms was an essential condition for the revival of the business unit. I told them literally: "How can we convince the board about the value of our existence within the corporate family if we don't believe in it ourselves?"

I look back with pleasure at our mission discussions. We developed there a feeling of "concord" that was necessary for taking a renovated perspective. Not only for managers, but for everyone involved. The discussions with the operators opened new dimensions. Their excellent skills were apparent. We learned that, in order to move the business unit to a higher level of performance, we did not need a revolutionary change. Building simply on the existing insights, but this time with empathy and intuition, could result in major improvements. It was the first time in the history of the business unit that a large section of the employees, together with management, were involved in answering the questions about what changes were needed and why. From these discussions a necessary change process emerged as "feasible" and "self-regulating" (self-initiating).

The parallel, more formal strategic analysis was intended to provide a factual and objective base for the acquired insights and action plans. This chosen method was standard practice in headquarters. The ensuing conclusions were by definition "trustworthy" for the decision-makers who had to reintegrate the business unit in the corporate family. Deviating from the traditional procedures of the concern, the report of the strategic deliberations was formulated in an understandable language by the "crew" itself. In this way the desired self-confidence and esteem became directly imbedded in the obtained strategic data. The business unit appeared after further study to be one of the best performing units of the concern. I took it to be my task to inform thoroughly all employees about these findings. In fact, the final report was already being discussed with all the people in the business unit before the final decision was taken to reintegrate us in the corporate family.

These periodical meetings with the total group of employees, in groups of about 20 persons, did turn into a tradition. The employees were and are thereby maximally informed about the developments of the business. The result was a foundation of shared common sense for desired or necessary adaptations. Such a foundation implied that the shared information was kept reliable and discussible. I requested the same openness from all the managers.

The presence of the consultant in the search conference enabled me to participate in the discussions in a normal way. In a way I was as equally interested and even curious as the other participants to hear the conclusions. The few times that I affirmed my views were on issues of social policy, safety, and ecology. The dominant open and free discussions made it possible for all members to assert their views and opinions. The work and reports of the subgroups clarified their opinions about entrepreneurial behaviour well.

THE FUTURE

The first results are in! Headquarters has accepted the strategic changes. The mission statement is alive. The "external bad guy" is gone; the business unit is now indeed in charge of its own future. What matters now is real collaboration. In the past year the principles of process-oriented organizations have been introduced in workshops. The mutual fine-tuning of the different functions within our business unit was central, as well as making the added value of each member involved explicit. Initiative and self-regulation served as key concepts. They are now also included in the performance reviews. The corporate culture is still largely technocratic, although positive changes become manifest. But we did pay a price for the pure instrumental approach towards our employees by previous management.

I hope to round off the next phase with an intensive training programme. All members of the business unit will be invited to these workshops in collaboration and policy-making. Ample attention will be given to create a "win–win" situation for the committed employees who actively contribute to the performance of the business unit. Their contributions will be appreciated and considered for their career development. Maximum utilization of the available knowledge and learning must guarantee a lasting commitment, based on a clear understanding of the business situation of XO.

EUROPEAN JOURNAL OF WORK AND ORGANIZATIONAL PSYCHOLOGY, 1999, 8 (1), 109–133

On Charisma and Need for Leadership

Reinout E. De Vries

Department of Management and Public Administration,
School of Social and Economic Development,
University of the South Pacific, Fiji

Robert A. Roe

Work and Organization Research Centre,
Tilburg University, The Netherlands

Tharsi C.B. Taillieu

Department of Work and Organizational Psychology
University of Leuven, Belgium

Some scholars have argued and found that the relationship between trans-formational or charismatic leadership and outcomes can be moderated by subordinate or situational characteristics (e.g. Bass & Avolio, 1990; Podsakoff, MacKenzie, & Bommer, 1996). Still, there is insufficient evidence on this issue. In this article we examine need for leadership (De Vries, 1997) as a moderator of the relation between a measure of charismatic leadership (Bass, 1985a; Den Hartog, Van Muijen, & Koopman, 1994) and subordinate outcomes. Need for leadership is found to moderate the relation between charismatic leadership and three out of four subordinate outcomes. Furthermore, we examine the relationship between charismatic leadership and need for leadership. Although it has been asserted that transformational or socialized charismatic leaders are able to empower and develop subordinates to become leaders themselves (e.g. Bass & Avolio, 1990; Kuhnert, 1994; Yammarino, 1994), we find a positive relationship between charismatic leadership and need for leadership, which suggests that subordinates are more, instead of less, dependent when a charismatic leader is present.

INTRODUCTION

One of the attributes which has often been associated with exceptional personal characteristics is *charisma*. Since 1977, several theories on charisma have been proposed, using terms such as "charismatic leadership" (Conger & Kanungo,

Requests for reprints should be addressed to R.E. De Vries, Department of Management and Public Administration, School of Social and Economic Development, University of the South Pacific, PO Box 1168, Suva, Fiji; email: devries_r@usp.ac.fj

House, 1977), "transforming leadership" (Burns, 1978), "transformational leadership" (Bass, 1985a, 1985b, 1990; Bass & Avolio, 1994), "visionary leadership" (Westley, 1991), "inspirational leadership" (Bass, 1988; Den Hartog, et al., 1994), or "change-centred leadership" (Ekvall, 1991; Ekvall & Arvonen, 1991). These theories focus on leaders who have an exceptional influence on the effort, motivation, and performance of subordinates. In this study we investigate the role of *need for leadership* (De Vries, 1997) in relation to charismatic leadership and outcomes. We examine how charisma relates to need for leadership, and whether need for leadership moderates the relationship between charisma and subordinate outcome variables. We will start with a brief overview of the research on charisma and an introduction of the "need for leadership" construct. Next, we will discuss the direct relationship of need for leadership and charismatic leadership and the possibility of a moderator effect. We will discuss our method of research, and, subsequently, present the results. Our article will finish with the conclusions and a discussion.

CHARISMA

Originally, charisma referred to individuals endowed with special qualities, standing out of the crowd. House (1977) specified various indicators of charismatic leadership involving follower perceptions, leader traits, and leader behaviour. Traits typical of charismatic leaders include a strong need for power, high self-confidence, and strong convictions. Need for power, for instance, was found to be a predictor of presidential charisma (House, Spangler, & Woycke 1991). The following behaviours were regarded to be typical of leaders: impression management, articulation of an appealing vision, communication of high expectations, and expression of confidence in followers.

Some scholars have abandoned the personal characteristics view of charismatic leadership. Bryman (1992) noted that the sheer variety of charismatic leaders made it impossible to single out special traits that were common to all. Although Bryman notes that highly charismatic leaders have often been described as having striking eyes, a powerful voice, an abundance of energy and confidence, and a capacity for empathy, none of these characteristics could be attributed to all charismatic leaders. In an investigation of the relation between personal characteristics (emotional coping, behavioural coping, abstract orientation, innovation, risk-taking, and use of humour) and transformational leadership using sales agents, it was found that none of the characteristics were consistently related to transformational leadership (Dubinsky, Yammarino, & Jolson, 1995). It is doubtful, though, whether in a population of sales managers, in contrast with a population of presidents, enough (variation in) charismatic behaviour is present. In a study using personality adjectives, charismatic leaders were perceived to differ significantly from non-charismatic leaders on a great number of personality adjectives (Atwater, Penn, & Rucker, 1991). Charismatic leaders, in contrast with non-charismatic leaders, were strongly characterized by personality adjectives such as dynamic, adventuresome, inspiring, enthusiastic, outgoing, zestful, sociable, insightful, imaginative, enterprising, secure, confident, wise, and competent.

Bass and Avolio (1994) make a distinction between four aspects of transformational leadership, namely, idealized influence (formerly charisma), intellectual stimulation, inspirational motivation, and individualized consideration. The Multifactor Leadership Questionnaire (MLQ) measures these four aspects together with three transactional factors (contingent reward, active management-by-exception, and passive management-by-exception) and laissez-faire (Bass & Avolio, 1995). Transactional leadership refers to the exchange or withholding of favours (clarifications, feedback, support) for subordinates' performance. Leaders who practise laissez-faire leadership basically abstain from trying to influence subordinates.

The MLQ is a widely used instrument. Its contents and empirical structure have been subject to discussion, however. Many MLQ items measuring charisma, for instance, have been defined in terms of their effects, augmenting the chance that high correlations with outcomes are obtained (Den Hartog, et al., 1994). Tepper and Percy (1994), using Confirmatory Factor Analysis (CFA) with a reduced MLQ version, found that two dimensions, one transformational and one transactional, captured the essence of the MLQ. In a CFA conducted by Bycio, Hackett, and Allen (1995), a two-factor solution, reflecting Active versus Passive leadership, was found to best represent the data obtained using the MLQ. Den Hartog, Van Muijen, and Koopman (1994, 1997) could not interpret an eight-factor solution in an explorative principal component analysis of the MLQ. A three-factor solution was proposed instead, comprising an inspirational leadership factor, a transactional leadership factor, and a passive leadership factor. Although Bass and Avolio (1993) maintain that a conceptual distinction can be made between the eight transformational and transactional factors, they admit that often transformational factors could not be distinguished empirically. Related to the behavioural point of view is the question of whether charismatic or transformational leadership can be learned. According to Avolio and Bass (1988), charisma is not an inborn trait, but is something that can be trained in a laboratory setting. Preliminary results from a study by Avolio and Bass (1995) showed a positive shift in inspirational motivation and intellectual stimulation rated by subordinates six months after a training programme was conducted. When participants had proposed changes, the effects were greater than when no change was proposed. However, no significant changes were observed in idealized influence (charisma) and individualized consideration.

Although the question remains whether charisma is something that resides in the person (House & Howell, 1992), whether it is a behavioural phenomenon (Conger & Kanungo, 1994), an aspect of social exchange (Bryman, 1992), or an attributional phenomenon (Lord & Maher, 1993), most researchers endorse the importance of charisma for organizational outcomes. Some studies have shown that this stance could only be supported if the same raters were used. This supports the view that charisma holds at an individual level of analysis but not at a dyad or group level (Yammarino & Dubinsky, 1994). Hater and Bass (1988), for instance, found that transformational leadership significantly added to the effectiveness of subordinates when subordinate ratings were used but not when supervisor ratings were used. Seltzer and Bass (1990) found that transformational leadership (but especially charisma) added 12% in leader effectiveness rated by subordinates to the variance explained by initiating structure and consideration; another 28% in subordinate's extra effort and another 8% in subordinate's satisfaction with the leader. These effects disappeared when a criss-cross design was employed. With different subordinates providing independent and dependent measures, transformational leadership only added an extra 6% of variance in leader effectiveness and 8% of variance in satisfaction with the leader. The explained variance was mainly brought about, though, by a negative relation of intellectual stimulation with the outcome variables, which did not conform to expectations. Charisma did not explain any additional variance in the outcomes.

In another study, it was found that charisma significantly added variance to contingent reward in explaining performance evaluation and recommended early promotion when a criss-cross design was used (Waldman, Bass, & Yammarino, 1990). Conversely, contingent reward did not add any variance to charisma in explaining the outcomes. In a longitudinal design in the US Navy, transformational leadership (i.e. one latent variable with charisma, individualized consideration, intellectual stimulation, and inspirational leadership as its indicators) was found to be related to objective as well as subjective performance evaluations, whereas transactional leadership was not related to any of these evaluations (Yammarino, Spangler, & Bass, 1993). Bycio et al. (1995) showed that, of all transformational leadership characteristics, charismatic leadership was the most important predictor of satisfaction with the leader, leader effectiveness, intent to leave, and organizational commitment.

While charisma seems to affect organizational and individual outcomes, it remains to be established how charisma relates to subordinate characteristics, and how its effectiveness depends on such characteristics. These questions are central in this article.

Only few studies have been conducted on the first question. Burns (1978) and Yukl (1989) argued that transformational or charismatic leadership can change the values, attitudes, assumptions, and behaviours of subordinates. Shamir, House, and Arthur (1993), for instance, proposed that charismatic leadership has an influence on subordinate's self-expression, self-esteem, self-consistency, identity, and faith. Podsakoff, MacKenzie, Moorman, and Fetter (1990) found that transformational leadership was positively related to subordinates' extra-role or "organizational citizenship behaviours" (OCBs). However, these effects were indirect. Transformational leadership was positively related to trust in the leader, which in its turn had a positive relation with the OCBs altruism, conscientiousness, courtesy, and sportsmanship, but not with civic virtue. Again, contrary to expectations, intellectual stimulation had a negative relation with a criterion, in this case, trust.

Even less research has been devoted to the second question. Podsakoff et al., (1996) proposed that subordinates' need for independence moderates the relation between intellectual stimulation and outcomes. They suggested that intellectual stimulation can be irritating and ineffective for subordinates with a high need for independence, while being effective for subordinates with a low need for independence. This proposition was not substantiated. The researchers did find a positive relation of intellectual stimulation with role conflict, which was moderated by professional orientation. With low professional orientation, intellectual stimulation was positively related to role conflict, whereas with high professional orientation there was no relation between intellectual stimulation and role conflict. They also found a moderator effect of group cohesiveness. At low levels of group cohesiveness, intellectual stimulation was negatively related to general satisfaction, while at high levels of group cohesiveness, intellectual stimulation was positively related to general satisfaction.

NEED FOR LEADERSHIP

In this study we focus on "need for leadership" (De Vries, 1997) as a characteristic of subordinates. Need for leadership differs from other relevant conceptualizations in the leadership domain because it is not an asset of the leader, but an asset of the subordinate in his or her situation, job, or organization. In this way, the concept of need for leadership fulfils the wish of scholars for a more follower-centred theory of leadership (Hollander & Offermann, 1990; Meindl, 1990; Mmobuosi, 1991). Leader-centred approaches have dominated the leadership research agenda with their focus on the personality traits, behavioural styles, and decision-making methods of the leader. According to Hollander and Offermann (1990), it has become important to incorporate the subordinates in leadership models in order to deepen our understanding of the leadership process. Meindl (1990) points at a lack of theories fitting leader traits and behaviours to the needs and personalities of subordinates. Need for leadership, with its focus on followers, may be a solution to the theoretical gap by filling this vacuum. We use the following definition: *Need for leadership is the extent to which an employee wishes the leader to facilitate the paths towards individual, group, and/or organizational goals.*

The need is not a basic need, such as the need for food or social contact, since it lacks the distinguishing feature of an urge that persists until gratification is achieved. It is rather a quasi-need in the sense of Lewin (1951), evoked in a particular setting. For this reason De Vries (1997, p. 93) speaks of need for leadership as a social-contextual motive. "Social" refers to the social setting in which the motive develops. People typically acquire new needs in group settings by means of socialization and acculturation processes. For example, a cohesive group may evoke or enhance the need for leadership among its members. "Contextual" refers to environmental contingencies of the need. Ryan (1995) argues that people may have different needs in different settings and/or at different times. People who are self-confident and capable in one setting may feel insecure and adroit in another. Need for leadership may thus become salient in work situations and reflect the organizational setting people are in, the type of work they perform, their tenure, etc.

The subordinate's need for leadership has different aspects. First of all, the subordinate may wish or may not wish a leader's intervention. The wish implies that the subordinate has positive feelings towards the contribution the leader is expected to make. The reverse, no wish, implies that the subordinate does not feel that the leader will make a contribution or even that the leader may hinder his or her goal achievement. Second, the facilitation of paths implies that the leader is seen as fulfilling certain functions which are instrumental and valuable in the subordinate's eyes. In the third place, the leader's influence contributes to the fulfilment of individual, group, and/or organizational goals. It should be noted that the organizational and group goals may or may not be compatible with the individual goals. Organizational and group goals may become individual goals when they are internalized by the subordinate. A *subjective* need for leadership is associated with individual goals; a more *objective* need for leadership is associated with group or organizational goals.

The relevance of need for leadership in research on charismatic leadership is obvious. We expect subordinates with a low need for leadership to act more or less independently, and to show little responsiveness to the interventions by their leaders. Subordinates with a high need for leadership, on the other hand, may be expected to subject themselves to the acts of the leader, and to contribute to the supervisor's image as a charismatic leader. A certain level of need for leadership might even be considered a prerequisite for the influence of charismatic leaders on their subordinates.

A number of studies have focused on constructs which resemble need for leadership. Most of the studies have paid little attention to the definition and operationalization of the proposed constructs. Furthermore, the subordinate leadership needs have usually been explored as part of a wider study. Consequently, the results have not been integrated in the mainstream of research on leadership. The studies can be roughly divided into two contrasting types: research on need for leadership and research on need for work without a leader. Examples of the first type are studies on need for closer supervision (Ashkanasy & Gallois, 1994), need for supervision (Martin, 1983), need for clarity (Keller, 1989), need for structure (Stoker & De Jong, 1996), and leadership need strength (Seers & Graen, 1984). Examples of the second type are studies on need for autonomy (Emans & Radstaak, 1990; Landeweerd & Boumans, 1994) and need for independence (Kerr & Jermier, 1978).

Most studies have investigated the effects of these "needs" on the relation of leadership with subordinate or organizational outcomes. Some studies have used subgrouping, comparing the relation of leadership and outcomes between groups high and groups low on the investigated "need". Others have used moderated multiple regression to find significant interactions between leadership and the "need". The findings of Keller (1989), Stoker and De Jong (1996), Emans and Radstaak (1990), and Landeweerd and Boumans (1994) point in the same direction, even though they suffered from methodological weaknesses resulting in low power. In those cases in which a significant moderator effect was detected, i.e. when employees needed clarity in their job or less autonomy, leadership was more strongly related to subordinate outcomes than in cases in which employees did not have such needs. The findings concerning need for independence (Kerr & Jermier, 1978) have been less clear. Need for independence did moderate the relation between several forms of leadership behaviour and criteria in six out of 82 (7.3%) cases (De Vries, 1997). There was no consistency, though, in the type of the moderator effect in these instances. In three of the cases, a negative (simple or pure) moderator effect was found, while in the other three cases a positive (simple or pure) moderator effect was found.

THE RELATIONSHIP BETWEEN CHARISMA AND NEED FOR LEADERSHIP

The first research question addressed in this article is: What is the relationship between charismatic leadership and need for leadership? Following Bass and Avolio (1990), Kuhnert (1994), and Yammarino (1994), employees with a transformational leader should show a lower need for leadership compared to employees with a non-transformational leader. Since charismatic leadership is an important part of transformational leadership, this line of argument would make one expect a negative correlation between the degree of charismatic leadership and the strength of the need for leadership. In another vein, one might argue that charismatic leadership may produce a stronger bond between the leader and subordinate, which may result in a higher need for leadership. Actually, Bass (1985a) acknowledges that charismatic leaders may keep followers weak and dependent. On this basis one would expect a positive correlation between charismatic leadership and need for leadership. Alternatively, one may conceive of a process in which the presence of subordinates with a higher need for leadership provides better chances for superiors to manifest themselves as charismatic leaders. Such a process would also result in a positive correlation between charismatic leadership and need for leadership, the causal order being reversed. And finally, of course, there is the possibility that these different processes take place simultaneously.

NEED FOR LEADERSHIP AS A MODERATOR

Although situational theories of leadership have been abundant, there has been a lack of research on the issue whether the relation between charismatic leadership and outcomes may be moderated by situational characteristics. Bass and Avolio (1990), for instance, propose that the relation between charismatic leadership and outcomes may be moderated by "crisis". In times of crisis, charismatic leaders may be more successful than in stable periods. The need for leadership among subordinates is another situational variable that may moderate the relationship between charismatic leadership and outcomes. Need for leadership qualifies as a potential moderator, since it is likely to capture the effects of other individual, task, and organizational characteristics (De Vries, 1997). Thus, we formulate our second research question as follows: Does need for leadership moderate the relation between charisma and outcome variables?

In our study, we focus on the following employees' outcomes: job satisfaction, organizational commitment, work stress, and role conflict. We expect charismatic leadership to be positively related to job satisfaction and organizational commitment. There is strong empirical evidence that these outcomes are positively related to transformational or charismatic leadership (e.g. Bycio et al., 1995; Den Hartog 1997; Podsakoff et al., 1996). We expect it to be negatively related to work stress and role conflict. The negative relation between role conflict and transformational leadership has been substantiated by Podsakoff et al. (1996). Need for leadership is expected to moderate the relation between charismatic leadership and outcomes in the following way: Among subordinates with a low need for leadership we expect the relation between charismatic leadership and outcomes to be weaker than among subordinates with a high need for leadership. Performance outcomes will not be considered in this study, since our sample did not permit objective and comparable performance criteria to be obtained.

METHOD

Sample

In order to maximize the power of our moderator analyses, we decided to draw a large sample of working people employed by different organizations. Thus, a random sample of 4523 Dutch households in Middle Brabant (a region in the province Noord-Brabant in The Netherlands) was selected from the telephone directory and contacted by telephone. Of these, 2000 households had one or more job-holders willing to participate, who subsequently received a questionnaire. A total of 958 questionnaires were returned. The average age of the respondents was 39.2 years (SD = 9.6), the mean tenure was 10.7 years (SD = 8.9). Of the 958 respondents 291 (30.4%) were female and 665 (69.4%) were male. The educational level of the respondents in the sample shows sufficient variation. In the sample, 3.4% completed junior high school, 15.4% completed high school, 14.7% completed lower occupational training, 34.1% completed middle occupational training, 24.3% completed higher occupational training, and 8.1% were university graduates.

In comparison with the national work force (Centraal Bureau voor Statistiek, 1996), the service sector is over-represented, although the branches of trade, hotels and restaurants, and banks and insurance are under-represented (Table 1). However, there seems to be a good match between the sample and the total Dutch population with regard to the labour force in farming, mining, industry, public utilities, construction, and transport and storage. The deviations of the sample from the national population were found to be significant ($\chi^2_{(8)} = 290.03$, $P < .001$). The sample deviated even more from the Middle Brabant labour force (Samenwerkingsverband Midden Brabant, 1996), notably with respect to industry, trade, hotels and restaurants, and service ($\chi^2_{(8)} = 543.98$, $P < .001$).[1] The number of respondents in industry matches the national population better than the Middle Brabant population. To obtain moderator effects, though, sufficient variation in business sector was found for the purpose of this study.

TABLE 1

Comparison of the Labour Force in The Netherlands, Middle Brabant, and the Sample

	National[a]		Middle Brabant[b]		Sample[c]	
Business Sector	N(1,000s)	%	N	%	N	%
Farming	103	1.7	715	0.5	25	2.6
Mining	9	0.2	5	0.0	2	0.2
Industry	1,016	17.0	34,992	23.3	161	6.9
Public utilities	43	0.7	587	0.4	20	2.1
Construction	353	5.9	9,157	6.1	88	9.3
Trade/hotels/restaurants	1,147	19.2	35,613	23.7	80	8.4
Transport and storage	388	6.5	7,760	5.2	34	3.6
Banks and insurance	950	15.9	13,200	8.8	50	5.3
Service	1,951	32.7	48,152	32.1	491	51.6
Total	5,960	100	150,181	100	951	100

[a]National statistics provided by the Central Office of Statistics, the Netherlands (Centraal Bureau voor Statistiek, 1996), taken in first semester, 1995. [b]Middle Brabant statistics provided by the Cooperation Middle Brabant (Samenwerkingsverband Midden Brabant, 1996), taken in May 1995. [c]Taken in February 1995.

[1]It should be noted that Pearsons' χ^2 is biased when expected frequencies are lower than 1. Compared with the value of the sample of 2, we find an expected frequency in the sample of 0.03 when using the Middle Brabant mining population. The squared difference $(2–0.03)^2$ of 3.88 is thus transformed to a χ^2-value of 129.33 after division through 0.03; which is already more than five times the critical ($P < .01$; $df = 8$) χ^2-value!

Instruments

Two different instruments have been used in the research on need for leadership, a subjective (the NL-S) and an objective part (the NL-O). The construction of the need for leadership instrument was conducted in three phases, a theoretical-rational phase, an internal-structural phase, and an external-criterion phase (Millon, 1983). In the first phase, the theoretical-rational phase, items were written on the basis of the theory involved. In this phase a judgement was made of the content of the items taking into account criteria regarding the level of complexity, the length, and the comprehensibility of the items. In the second phase, the internal-structural phase, scales from the items were tested on their internal homogeneity. Factor-analyses and reliability analyses were part of this phase. In the third phase, the external-criterion phase, the scales were correlated with external criteria, to evaluate their (convergent and discriminant) validity. Both the NL-S and the NL-O contained adequate reliability and validity. In this study the NL-S has a Cronbach alpha of 0.93 and the NL-O of 0.94. The instruments are fully described in De Vries (1997).

The scale measuring charismatic leadership is a reduced version of Bass's (1985a) scale measuring transformational leadership. Den Hartog et al. (1994, 1997) factor-analysed a 40-item Dutch version of the transformational leadership scales. The first factor contained 18 items and represented inspirational leadership. This scale had a Cronbach alpha of 0.95. Eleven items with high item-total correlations were selected for the scale used in our study. We renamed the scale "charismatic leadership", because the items strongly resemble the items derived from the first factor in Bass's (1985a, pp. 207–210) original factor analysis of the transformational leadership scales, which was originally named "charismatic leadership". In our study this scale has an alpha of 0.93. It should be noted that the items representing charismatic leadership describe different domains. In contrast with human- and task-oriented leadership, which clearly describe leadership behaviours, some of the charismatic leadership items resemble personality traits (e.g. "My supervisor projects a powerful, dynamic and magnetic presence"), some describe behaviours (e.g. "My supervisor mobilizes a collective sense of mission"), some describe subordinate affects (e.g. "I have complete confidence in my supervisor"), and some describe subordinate perceptions (e.g. "In my mind, my supervisor is a symbol of success and accomplishment").

The employee outcome variables used in this study are: job satisfaction, organizational commitment, work stress, and role conflict. As indicated in Table 2, the reliabilities of these outcome variables are adequate, ranging from 0.75 for role conflict to 0.81 for job satisfaction. The instruments for job satisfaction, organizational commitment, and work stress have been obtained from Taillieu (1987) and were further refined and extensively described in the insurance company study (Taillieu & De Vries, 1995; Taillieu, Van der Wielen, De Vries,

& Dikschei, 1993) and in De Vries (1997). The job satisfaction scale contains 11 items. It consists of items which denote the degree of satisfaction derived from the level of variation, autonomy, responsibility in the job, career possibilities, salary, and interaction with colleagues. An example of an item is: "I am satisfied with the amount of variation in my job". The scale has a Cronbach alpha of 0.81.

The scale for organizational commitment consists of six items. Examples of items used are: "I would change company, if another were to offer me a higher salary" (reversely scored), "I feel at home in my company", and "I praise my organization when talking to acquaintances". The scale has a Cronbach alpha of 0.78. The scale for work stress consists of seven items as used in the cross-sectional study. Examples of items are: "I have to hurry to finish my work in time", "I often cannot cope with the amount of work", "This work is putting a strain on my health", and "This work requires a great deal of effort". The scale has a Cronbach alpha of 0.77.

Role conflict was measured using the instrument of Rizzo, House, and Lirtzman (1970). Role conflict is viewed in terms of incompatibility between organizational demands and own values, problems of personal resource allocation, conflict between obligations to several other people, and conflict between excessively numerous or difficult tasks. The scale consists of eight items. Alpha coefficients reported range from 0.56 to 0.82 (Cook, Hepworth, Wall, & Warr, 1981). In our cross-sectional study the scale has a Cronbach alpha of 0.75.

Analyses

To obtain the relation between charismatic leadership and need for leadership, we computed Pearson correlations between the variables. To find moderator effects we used a modified version of the Hierarchical or Moderated Multiple

TABLE 2
Number of Items, Means, Standard Deviations, and
Cronbach Alphas of the Main Scales in Our Study

	No.[a] of items	Cronbach α	Mean	SD
Charismatic leadership	11	0.93	32.40	9.30
Need for leadership (NL-S)	17	0.93	44.69	13.65
Need for leadership (NL-O)	17	0.94	56.28	14.06
Job satisfaction	11	0.81	42.60	6.38
Organizational commitment	6	0.78	22.02	5.25
Work stress	7	0.77	21.12	5.12
Role conflict	8	0.75	19.48	5.45

[a]Likert (1–5) completely disagree–completely agree scales were used.

Regression (MMR) procedure suggested by Howell, Dorfman, and Kerr (1986). The following regression model was tested:

$$y = \beta_0 + \beta_1 x + \beta_2 z + \beta_3 xz + \varepsilon$$

in which y stands for the criteria (i.e. job satisfaction, organizational commitment, work stress, and role conflict), x for charismatic leadership, z for need for leadership, and xz for the interaction between charismatic leadership and need for leadership. Using the standardized regression values of need for leadership (β_2) and the interaction term (β_3) we can specify the type of effect of need for leadership when charismatic leadership (β_1) is either positively, negatively, or not related to the criterion (De Vries, 1997). In the presentation of our research findings we will only include data using the NL-S. It should be noted that similar results were obtained using the NL-O.

RESULTS

Correlations

In Table 3 the results of our correlational analysis are shown. As one can see, charismatic leadership is positively correlated to both need for leadership scales. It appears that employees with charismatic leaders have a higher need for leadership than those with leaders low on charisma. This is contrary to the expectations of leadership scholars, who argue that charismatic leadership reduces the dependency of subordinates by empowering them. Furthermore, charismatic leadership is positively related to job satisfaction and organizational commitment, and negatively related to work stress and role conflict. The sub-

TABLE 3
The Correlation between the (Need for) Leadership Scales and the Criteria

	Charisma	NL-S	NL-O	Job Satisfaction	Organizational Commitment	Work Stress	Role Conflict
Charisma	1.00						
NL-S	0.24**	1.00					
NL-O	0.21**	0.63**	1.00				
Job satisfaction	0.48**	0.00	0.01	1.00			
Organizational commitment	0.46**	0.06	0.04	0.72**	1.00		
Work stress	−0.09*	0.05	0.12**	−0.21**	−0.24**	1.00	
Role conflict	−0.15**	0.06	0.12**	−0.28**	−0-.36**	0.59**	1.00

$*P < .05; **P < .01.$

jective and objective need for leadership scales are strongly correlated to each other. Of the two need for leadership scales, only NL-O shows a weak positive correlation with the outcome variables work stress and role conflict. This indicates that when subordinates perceive a leader to be needed in their type of work, they are somewhat more troubled by work stress and role conflict. Last of all, the criteria are modestly to strongly correlated to each other.

Moderator Effects

The results of the hierarchical MMRs are shown in Table 4. In the table, the criteria are regressed on charismatic leadership, need for leadership, and their interaction term. The relations between charismatic leadership and the criteria are moderated in three out of four cases. In the case of job satisfaction and organizational commitment, a low need for leadership is associated with a weaker relation between charismatic leadership and criteria than a high need for leadership. The negative relation between charismatic leadership and work stress is not moderated by need for leadership. Need for leadership does act as a

TABLE 4
Moderated Multiple Regression of Criteria on Charismatic Leadership,
Need for Leadership (NL-S), and Their Interaction

Variable	R^2_{adj}	ΔR^2	$\%^a$	Δf^b	β^c
Criterion: Job satisfaction					
Charismatic leadership	0.23	0.23	92.6	220.58	0.52***
Need for leadership	0.24	0.01	4.7	11.27	−0.11***
Interaction	0.25	0.01	2.7	6.64	0.08*
Criterion: Organizational commitment					
Charismatic leadership	0.22	0.23	94.4	214.01	0.50***
Need for leadership	0.23	0.00	1.9	4.37	−0.07*
Interaction	0.24	0.01	3.7	8.54	0.09**
Criterion: Work stress					
Charismatic leadership	0.01	0.01	51.7	7.70	−0.12***
Need for leadership	0.02	0.01	42.3	6.38	0.10*
Interaction	0.02	0.00	6.0	0.88	−0.03
Criterion: Role conflict					
Charismatic leadership	0.03	0.03	61.2	20.08	−0.20***
Need for leadership	0.03	0.01	22.0	7.28	0.10**
Interaction	0.04	0.01	16.7	5.57	−0.09*

[a]% of net explained variance explained by particular independent variable; [b]when $F > 3.84$, $P < .05$; when $F > 6.63$, $P < .01$. [c]fully standardized final βs; i.e. when all variables are in the equation.
*$P < .05$, **$P < .01$, ***$P < .001$.

moderator of the negative relation of charismatic leadership to role conflict. With a low need for leadership, again, the relation between charismatic leadership and role conflict is weaker than with a high need for leadership. The first research question can thus be answered positively. In three out of four cases (low) need for leadership makes the relation between charismatic leadership and criteria less strong.

CONCLUSIONS AND DISCUSSION

Our results show that charismatic leadership and need for leadership are related to each other. Subordinates with charismatic leaders have a higher need for leadership than subordinates with noncharismatic leaders. Furthermore, need for leadership moderated the relation between charismatic leadership and three of our four outcome variables. A lower need for leadership was associated with a weaker relation between charismatic leadership and the outcome variables in our study.

Our findings seem to contradict the ideas about transformational leadership and socialized charisma, but some clarifications on charismatic and transformational leadership concepts on the one hand, and personalized and socialized charisma on the other, are needed before we can conclude that this really is the case. First of all, when looking at the similarities and differences between charismatic and transformational leadership, according to Bass (1985a), charisma is a necessary, but not sufficient, component of transformational leadership. Although, just as charismatic leaders, transformational leaders may arouse strong emotions and identification, they may also serve as a coach, mentor or teacher of subordinates. Transformational leaders may make subordinates independent from the leaders by empowering them (Kuhnert, 1994; Yammarino, 1994). According to Yammarino (1994, p. 46), "Ultimately, the most successful transformational leaders, regardless of organizational level, are those who have made their followers, colleagues, and even superiors ... leaders in their own right".[2] Kuhnert (1994, p. 23) even sees it as a moral responsibility of leaders to develop their subordinates. In his words, "leaders must aspire to more than just getting others to follow: They must see the development of their associates as their personal responsibility if the organization is to grow and maximize its potential". In other words, charisma itself seems to be neutral with respect to subordinate empowerment while transformational leadership should lead to subordinate development and empowerment.

Second, a distinction has been made between personalized and socialized charisma. Leaders who are exemplified by their personalized (rather than socialized) charisma resist empowering subordinates in order to maintain their

---

[2]In fact, this implies that room is left for unsuccessful transformational leaders, who do not turn followers into leaders.

own base of power (Howell, 1988, in Bass & Avolio, 1990). Bass and Avolio (1990, p. 242) state that "Transformational leaders, although viewed as charismatic, gain greater levels of long-term performance by developing followers to a higher level of autonomy." This would imply that transformational leaders show socialized charisma, which results in empowered subordinates. Personalized charisma, on the other hand, results in greater subordinate dependency and less empowerment. With empowerment, dependency, or need for leadership as a criterion, we could construct the following three clusters of charismatic leaders. On the one side are personalized charismatics, who have dependent subordinates with a high need for leadership; in the middle are "neutral" charismatics, whose subordinates are neither dependent nor independent; and on the other side are socialized charismatics or transformational leaders, who have empowered subordinates with a low need for leadership.

Given these distinctions, our results can be explained in different ways. First, we may have measured personalized charisma, and the findings are in line with expectations. Second, we may have measured "neutral" charisma or even socialized (transformational) charisma, and the findings are not in line with expectations. Third, it could be argued that need for leadership is different from empowerment and subordinate (in-)dependency, and that no conclusion can be reached. The last explanation can be ruled out, as De Vries (1997) has shown that need for leadership is negatively related to subordinate experience and need for independence. Furthermore, need for leadership has been validated with Martin's (1983) changes in supervision. The more subordinates were willing to work independently without a supervisor, the lower their need for leadership. As a result, we believe that empowered subordinates have a lower need for leadership. The first possibility can be discarded as well. It does not seem likely that we have measured personalized charisma as the items are derived from the transformational factor of Bass's Multifactor Leadership Questionnaire (Den Hartog et al., 1997). The items used in our study resemble the items from Bass's (1985a) original charismatic leadership scale, and they are part of the transformational scales in later studies of Bass and co-workers. Consequently, it would seem as if we have measured socialized charisma or transformational leadership instead. However, close scrutiny of the items reveals that they are neutral with respect to the motivation and goals (socialized or personalized) of the leader, which suggests that we have measured "neutral" charisma. Still, "neutral" charisma is related to a stronger need for leadership, which may be contrary to expectations of transformational leadership researchers. Whether socialized (transformational) leadership itself is actually related to a stronger need for leadership is a subject of further study.

Some other issues should be raised in considering the results of this study. In the first place, we cannot be absolutely sure about the exact nature of the relationship between charismatic leadership and need for leadership. Viewed from a behavioural perspective, charismatic leadership can instil a higher need in subordinates. There may also be some reciprocity between these two variables. With a higher need for leadership, subordinates may also attribute more charisma to their leader, as would be suggested by attributional theorists. A longitudinal study should help to ascertain which of these propositions is closer to the truth. In the second place, the significant interaction effects found accounted for an average of only 1% of the total variance in the criterion. We should be wary, though, in dismissing a finding like this as insignificant. According to Cohen (1988), an explained variance of 1% is small, yet it is approximately equivalent to the difference in mean height between 15- and 16-year old girls. Since most of the effect sizes of the leader characteristics on the criteria are small to medium in size, with a relation hovering on the average between 0.2 and 0.3, an interaction effect accounting for 1% of the variance also means that for subjects scoring very low on the moderator, there is virtually no relation between the predictor and the criterion, whereas at high scores, the relation between the predictor and criterion is very strong (i.e. approximately 0.4 to 0.5).

REFERENCES

Ashkanasy, N.M., & Gallois, C. (1994). Leader attributions and evaluations: Effects of locus of control, supervisory control, and task control. *Organizational Behaviour and Human Decision Processes, 59*, 27–50.

Atwater, L., Penn, R., & Rucker, L. (1991). Personal qualities of charismatic leaders. *Leadership and Organization Development Journal, 12*, 7–10.

Avolio, B.J., & Bass, B.M. (1988). Transformational leadership, charisma, and beyond. In J.G. Hunt, B.R. Baliga, H.P. Dachler, & C.A. Schriesheim (Eds.), *Emerging leadership vistas: International leadership symposia series* (pp. 29–49). Lexington, MA: Lexington Books/D.C. Heath & Co.

Avolio, B.J., & Bass, B.M. (1995). *You can bring a horse to water, but you can't make it drink: Evaluating a full range leadership model for training and development.* Unpublished manuscript, State University of New York, Binghamton, USA.

Bass, B.M. (1985a). *Leadership and performance beyond expectations.* New York: Free Press.

Bass, B.M. (1985b). Leadership: Good, better, best. *Organizational Dynamics, Winter*, 26–40.

Bass, B.M. (1988). The inspirational processes of leadership. *Journal of Management Development, 7*, 21–31.

Bass, B.M. (1990). *Bass and Stogdill's handbook of leadership: Theory, research and managerial applications.* New York: The Free Press.

Bass, B.M., & Avolio, B.J. (1990). The implications of transactional and transformational leadership for individual, team, and organizational development. In W. Pasmore & R.W. Woodman (Eds.), *Research in organizational change and development, Vol. 4* (pp. 231-272). Greenwich, CT: JAI Press.

Bass, B.M., & Avolio, B.J. (1993). Transformational leadership: A response to critiques. In M.M. Chemers & R. Ayman (Eds.), *Leadership theory and research: Perspectives and directions* (pp. 49–80). San Diego, CA: Academic Press.

Bass, B.M., & Avolio, B.J. (1994). *Improving organizational effectiveness through transformational leadership.* Thousand Oaks, CA: Sage Publications.

Bass, B.M., & Avolio, B.J. (1995). *Multifactor Leadership Questionnaire (MLQ) profile.* Binghamton, NY: State University of New York.

Bryman, A. (1992). *Charisma and leadership in organizations.* London: Sage.

Burns, J.M. (1978). *Leadership*. New York: Harper & Row.

Bycio, P., Hackett, R.D., & Allen, J.S. (1995). Further assessments of Bass's (1985) conceptualization of transactional and transformational leadership. *Journal of Applied Psychology, 80*, 468–478.

Centraal Bureau voor Statistiek (1996). *Statistisch jaarboek 1996*. 's-Gravenhage: SDU.

Cohen, J. (1988). *Statistical power analysis for the behavioural sciences*. Hillsdale, NJ: Lawrence Erlbaum Associates Inc.

Conger, J.A., & Kanungo, R.N. (1994). Charismatic leadership in organizations: Perceived behavioural attributes and their measurement. *Journal of Organizational Behaviour, 15*(5), 439–452.

Cook, J.D., Hepworth, S.J., Wall, T.D., & Warr, P.B. (1981). *The experience of work: A compendium and review of 249 measures and their use*. London: Academic Press.

De Vries, R.E. (1997). *Need for leadership: A solution to empirical problems in situational theories of leadership*. Doctoral dissertation, Tilburg University. Enschede, The Netherlands: FEBO Print.

Den Hartog, D.N. (1997). *Inspirational leadership*. Doctoral dissertation, Free University Amsterdam: Enschede, The Netherlands: Ipskamp BV. Printpartners.

Den Hartog, D.N., Van Muijen, J., & Koopman, P. (1994). Transactioneel versus transformationeel leiderschap: Een analyse van de MLQ in de Nederlandse situatie. *Gedrag en Organisatie, 7*, 155–166.

Den Hartog, D.N., Van Muijen, J.J., & Koopman, P.L. (1997). Transactional versus transformational leadership: An analysis of the MLQ. *Journal of Occupational and Organizational Psychology, 70*(1), 19–34.

Dubinsky, A.J., Yammarino, F.J., & Jolson, M.A. (1995). An examination of linkages between personal characteristics and dimensions of transformational leadership. *Journal of Business and Psychology, 9*, 315–335.

Ekvall, G. (1991). Change-centred leaders: Empirical evidence of a third dimension of leadership. *Leadership and Organization Development Journal, 12*(6), 18–23.

Ekvall, G., & Arvonen, J. (1991). Change-centered leadership: An extension of the two-dimensional model. *Scandinavian Journal of Management, 7*, 17–26.

Emans, B., & Radstaak, G. (1990). De rol van leidinggevenden bij verschillende niveaus van taakverruiming: Onderzoek op een aantal verpleegafdelingen van een ziekenhuis. *Gedrag en Organisatie, 3*(5), 376–392.

Hater, J.J., & Bass, B.M. (1988). Superiors' evaluations and subordinates' perceptions of transformational and transactional leadership. *Journal of Applied Psychology, 73*, 695–702.

Hollander, E.P., & Offermann, L.R. (1990). Power and leadership in organizations: Relationships in transition. *American Psychologist, 45*, 179–189.

House, R.J. (1977). A 1976 theory of charismatic leadership. In J.G. Hunt & L.L. Larson (Eds.), *Leadership: The cutting edge* (pp. 189–207). Carbondale, IL: Southern Illinois University Press.

House, R.J., & Howell, J.M. (1992). Personality and charismatic leadership. *Leadership Quarterly, 3*, 81–108.

House, R.J., Spangler, W.D., & Woycke, J. (1991). Personality and charisma in the US presidency: A psychological theory of leader effectiveness. *Administrative Science Quarterly, 36*, 364–396.

Howell, J.M. (1988). Two faces of charisma: Socialized and personalized leadership in organizations. In J.A. Conger & R.N. Kanungo (Eds.), *Charismatic leadership: The elusive factor in organizational effectiveness*. San Francisco: Jossey-Bass.

Howell, J.P., Dorfman, P.W., & Kerr, S. (1986). Moderator variables in leadership research. *Academy of Management Review, 11*, 88–102.

Keller, R.T. (1989). A test of the path-goal theory of leadership with need for clarity as a moderator in research and development organizations. *Journal of Applied Psychology, 74*, 208–212.

Kerr, S., & Jermier, J.M. (1978). Substitutes for leadership: Their meaning and measurement. *Organizational Behaviour and Human Performance, 22*, 375–403.

Kuhnert, K.W. (1994). Transforming leadership: Developing people through delegation. In B.M. Bass & B.J. Avolio (Eds.), *Improving organizational effectiveness through transformational leadership* (pp. 10–25). Thousand Oaks, CA: Sage Publications.

Landeweerd, J.A., & Boumans, N.P.G. (1994). The effect of work dimensions and need for autonomy on nurses' work satisfaction and health. *Journal of Occupational and Organizational Psychology, 67*, 207–217.

Lewin, K. (1951). *Field theory in social science: Selected theoretical papers.* New York: Harper & Row.

Lord, R.G., & Maher, K.J. (1993). *Leadership and information processing: Linking perceptions and performance.* New York: Routledge.

Martin, S. (1983). *Managing without managers: Alternative work arrangements in public organizations.* Beverly Hills, CA: Sage Publications.

Meindl, J.R. (1990). On leadership: An alternative to the conventional wisdom. In B.M. Staw & L.L. Cummings (Eds.), *Research in organizational behaviour, Vol. 12* (pp. 159–203). Greenwich, CT: JAI Press.

Millon, T. (1983). *Millon Multiracial Clinical Inventory Manual.* Minneapolis, MN: National Computer Systems.

Mmobuosi, I.B. (1991). Followership behaviour: A neglected aspect of leadership studies. *Leadership and Organization Development Journal, 12*, 11–16.

Podsakoff, P.M., MacKenzie, S.B., & Bommer, W.H. (1996). Transformational leader behaviours and substitutes for leadership as determinants of employee satisfaction, commitment, trust, and organizational citizenship behaviours. *Journal of Management, 22*, 259–298.

Podsakoff, P.M., MacKenzie, S.B., Moorman, R.H., & Fetter, R. (1990). Transformational leader behaviours and their effects on followers' trust in leader, satisfaction, and organizational citizenship behaviours. *Leadership Quarterly, 1*, 107–142.

Rizzo, J., House, R.J., & Lirtzman, S.I. (1970). Role conflict and ambiguity in complex organizations. *Administrative Science Quarterly, 15*, 150–163.

Ryan, R.M. (1995). Psychological needs and the facilitation of integrative processes. *Journal of Personality, 63*(3), 397–427.

Samenwerkingsverband Midden Brabant (1996). *Rapportage werkgelegenheidsenquete 1995.* Tilburg: SMB/Bureau IAP.

Seers, A., & Graen, G.B. (1984). The dual attachment concept: A longitudinal investigation of the combination of task characteristics and leader–member exchange. *Organizational Behaviour and Human Performance, 33*, 283–306.

Seltzer, J., & Bass, B.M. (1990). Transformational leadership: Beyond initiation and consideration. *Journal of Management, 16*, 693–703.

Shamir, B., House, R.J., & Arthur, M.B. (1993). The motivational effects of charismatic leadership: A self-concept based theory. *Organization Science, 4*, 577–594.

Stoker, J., & De Jong, R. (1996). Leidinggeven aan zelfstandige taakgroepen. *Gedrag en Organisatie, 9*(6), 401–415.

Taillieu, T.C.B. (1987). *Meaning of work: Relationships between personal and contextual factors.* Oisterwijk, The Netherlands: Research Meeting for the European Committee for Work and Pay.

Taillieu, T.C.B., & De Vries, R.E. (1995). *De arbeidsbeleving van de verzekeringsadviseur bij RVS-Rotterdam.* Tilburg, The Netherlands: Tilburg University.

Taillieu, T.C.B., Van der Wielen, J.M.M., De Vries, R.E., & Dikschei, G.M.D.M. (1993). *De arbeidsbeleving van de verzekeringsadviseur.* Tilburg, The Netherlands: Tilburg University.

Tepper, B.J., & Percy, P.M. (1994). Structural validity of the Multifactor Leadership Questionnaire. *Educational and Psychological Measurement, 54*, 734–744.

Waldman, D.A., Bass, B.M., & Yammarino, F.J. (1990). Adding to contingent-reward behaviour: The augmenting effect of charismatic leadership. *Group and Organization Studies, 15*, 381–394.

Westley, F. (1991). Bob Geldof and Live Aid: The affective side of global social innovation. *Human Relations, 44*, 1011–1036.

Yammarino, F.J. (1994). Indirect leadership: Transformational leadership at a distance. In B.M. Bass & B.J. Avolio (Eds.), *Improving organizational effectiveness through transformational leadership* (pp. 26–47). Thousands Oaks, CA: Sage Publications.

Yammarino, F.J., & Dubinsky, A.J. (1994). Transformational leadership theory: Using levels of analysis to determine boundary conditions. *Personnel Psychology, 47*, 787–811.

Yammarino, F.J., Spangler, W.D., & Bass, B.M. (1993). Transformational leadership and performance: A longitudinal investigation. *Leadership Quarterly, 4*, 81–102.

Yukl, G. (1989). Managerial leadership: A review of theory and research. *Journal of Management, 15*, 251–289.

Charisma and Need for Leadership Revisited

James G. Hunt, Institute for Leadership Research,
Texas Tech University USA

A Commentary on "On Charisma and Need for Leadership"
by Reinout de Vries, Robert Roe, and Tharsi Taillieu

Half a century ago Irving Knickerbocker (1948) set forth a leadership conceptualization based on leadership and follower need satisfaction. Hunt (1957) proposed an empirical work related to Knickerbocker's conceptual notion. In the 1960s, Beer (1966) conducted an empirical study relating several dimensions of leadership to various aspects of the need satisfaction of followers. The latest transfiguration of this leadership and needs linkage appears in the need for leadership concept articulated in the present article.

This long-standing intuitive appeal of notions related to need for leadership is also shown by the earlier literature emphasizing follower leadership preferences, either implicitly or explicitly (e.g. Fleishman, 1973; House, 1973; House, Filley, & Gujarati, 1971; Nealey & Blood, 1968). Indeed, Yukl (1971) formulated a model which postulated that follower satisfaction with the leader would be a function of the difference between a follower's leadership preference and the leader's behaviour. That model was related to the more general attitudinal discrepancy models of that time proposed by a number of investigators (e.g. Porter, 1962; Wood, 1970).

Such preferences studies go back as far as the late 1950s (e.g. Hemphill, 1957) although their heyday was in the 1960s and early 1970s. Some of the studies used discrepancy scores similar to the Yukl model above (e.g. Beer, 1966; Hemphill, 1957). Others treated preference and behaviour interactively in a manner similar to the current need for leadership study (e.g. Foa, 1957; Mannheim, Rim, & Grinberg, 1967). Finally, in the early 1970s, Hunt and Liebscher (1973) did a study comparing different discrepancy models with an interactive preference model and with a simple model of perceived behaviour with no preferences. Ultimately usage of these kinds of models faded as statistical problems with discrepancy scores became more obvious (e.g. Edwards, 1994). However, the more general underlying notion appears alive and well in its newly emerging need for leadership form.

Aside from my retrospective perspective, which I like to emphasize in commentaries such as this, my next thought was that the need for leadership concept was probably not broad enough—it needed to be embedded in one of the leadership contingency approaches. Substitutes for leadership (e.g. Kerr & Jermier, 1978) immediately came to mind, followed shortly by path-goal theory (e.g. House, 1973, 1996) and situational leadership theory (Hersey & Blanchard, 1984). Relatedly, but with a charismatic twist, Meindl's romance of leadership notion and RLS (Romance of Leadership) measure (Meindl & Ehrlich, 1988) entered my thoughts, as did the work of Hunt, Boal, and Dodge (1997).

However, I was fortunate enough to have a copy of De Vries' (1997) dissertation at hand and quickly discovered that in that dissertation, though not in the present article, most of these models had already been considered. Indeed, De Vries developed a conceptual model that did the very kind of embedding that first crossed my mind. It focused on follower task and organizational characteristics as these predicted the need for leadership and criteria and then related the need for leadership to leadership itself, reciprocally, and interactively between leadership and criteria. In so doing, the model set the stage for showing the role of need for leadership and various aspects of leadership substitutes as well as providing a broad gauge contingency framework allowing for numerous variables. Need for leadership provides a less abstract explanatory mechanism than has previously been used in the substitutes literature (see Hunt, 1991; Yukl, 1998, for the role of level of abstraction in the leadership literature).

Since this model has already been treated at great length in the dissertation, I will not rehash that here, even though the dissertation model did not emphasize charismatic leadership per se. What I will do is focus on a number of points raised by the current article either explicitly or implicitly in the charismatic context. I think these, rather than the 1% incremental criterion variance, are the concept's major contribution, just as I think reinvigoration of the field has been transformational/charismatic leadership's major contribution to the leadership area—even more than specific findings (Hunt, 1998).

DISCUSSION POINTS

For openers I couldn't help thinking about Meindl's (1990) notion of the romance of leadership, mentioned earlier. The authors mention Meindl's "follower-centered theory of leadership" and its consistency with their need for leadership concept. An important part of Meindl's approach has been his RLS instrument. This instrument essentially focuses on the extent to which followers attribute important occurrences to leadership as opposed to other causal agents. De Vries (1997) briefly mentions the romance of leadership notion in his dissertation but links it only indirectly with need for leadership. Here I am proposing that the relationship between need for leadership and romance of leadership be further explored, both conceptually and empirically using each of the scales. The RLS scale has begun to attract the attention of scholars beyond Meindl and its linkage with need for leadership seems natural, to me. Such work, among other things, could shed additional light on the follower-centric situational leadership model concerns of the present authors.

In a similar manner, I was struck by De Vries' (1997) discussion of Hersey and Blanchard's (1984) situational leadership model in his dissertation (although it was not mentioned in the current article). The model essentially argues that follower maturity moderates the response to leadership. The approach has been extremely popular among practitioners (Yukl, 1998) and, like preference approaches, has considerable intuitive appeal. However, there has not been much empirical work and what has been done has not been very supportive.

Need for leadership seems to me to provide a potentially more operational way to get at a concept similar to that of maturity (which does not have the careful empirical work that has gone into the need for leadership scale). What is really needed is a dynamic or at least a comparative statics longitudinal approach (e.g. Hunt, 1991). The dynamic approach is similar to a motion picture where the temporal process in moving from one time period to another is the central focus (Hunt, 1991, p. 280). The comparative statics approach is similar to a series of snapshots with the time periods between clearly identified (Hunt, 1991, p. 279). Either longitudinal approach also would call for modified conceptualization based on charismatic or transformational leadership as opposed to the task and relations dimensions in the original model. However, particularly if we think temporally and in terms of transformational leadership, such conceptualization and empirical work seems readily doable using the need for leadership scales in place of maturity.

Still another point, and one that pervades the charisma and transformational literature in general, is concerned with the criteria. Here, and in the broader literature, criteria seem to be used almost indiscriminately. It is almost as if charisma will predict any criterion equally well. In the present study there is some discrimination between satisfaction/involvement and stress/conflict. However, underdeveloped is the conceptualization concerning the specifics of why these specific criteria were chosen and how and why they should be related to charisma and need for leadership. Missing here, of course, is any semblance of an effectiveness measure and how, specifically, need for leadership should help charisma to predict these. Although the authors indicate an awareness of this lack of an effectiveness measure in their study, future work needs to address this concern. Along with effectiveness, it would be useful to use such measures as turnover and absenteeism, commitment, and other aspects of human resource maintenance criteria (Hunt, 1991). A number of these have been used in the transformational literature (Lowe, Kroeck, & Sivasubramaniam, 1996).

At the same time, both the literature and the authors tend to treat the kinds of criteria used here as if they were independent. The authors' correlation matrix shows varying relationships among these from moderate to strong. For some of our work we took commonly used measures in the charisma literature and found that factor analyses reduced the number of criteria considerably (see Hunt & Boal, 1996). The point here is that many criteria treated separately in the literature are really interrelated. I conclude from all of this that, future work should focus on an underlying framework relating criteria to each other and showing linking mechanisms among charisma, need for leadership, and the classes of criteria.

Related to the above arguments is a model called the "individual performance equation" by John Schermerhorn and colleagues (e.g. Martin, Schermerhorn, & Larson, 1989; Schermerhorn, Hunt, & Osborn, 1991), based on related work. The importance of that model here and for charismatic leadership in general is that it starts with a focus on performance and then works back to consideration of follower capacity, willingness, and opportunity to perform. Each of these three areas includes a number of aspects, and different components of leadership enter into the areas as appropriate. In some ways this model is not unlike the dissertation model mentioned earlier but, as indicated, one critical difference is the current model's performance orientation and those aspects of the setting required to obtain it.

An additional point is raised by the authors and seems to be of increasing importance in the literature. That point concerns charisma, transformation, and empowerment. The authors do a nice job of focusing on this issue and, in effect, deriving a simple three-cluster model of personalized charismatics with dependent followers, neutral charismatics with neither dependent nor independent followers, and socialized leaders (termed "transformational" by the authors) with empowered followers possessing a low need for leadership. Here, it seems to me as the authors suggest, that their construct can help shed light on this increasingly important topic, where the focus has ranged from autocratic charismatics to empowering ones, and from positive charismatics to negative charismatics. (For more on this topic, see Bass, 1990; Yukl, 1998.)

Another point concerns the question of the specificity of the need for leadership measure. This is a point that De Vries (1997)himself raises in his dissertation. It seems quite reasonable, as he argues there, to start with an overall measure such as reported there and here. Ultimately, one may want to consider such aspects as a need for charisma, a need for structure, a need for supportiveness, and the like. Interestingly, such a breakdown would lead one closer to the preference models mentioned earlier. While such models are not generally used any longer, per se, their reincarnation in need for leadership measures might be a useful move.

A final point, for me, that this article suggests both implicitly and explicitly, is the question of additional charismatic moderators. The authors argue that there is very little in the literature on this. I would agree, but would add some of the suggestions made by Bryman (1992) and even more detailed ones by Pawar and Eastman (1997). These latter authors do a thorough review of the literature, including much macro- and some micro-literature and develop a proposed set of "preliminary contextual factors". The authors cover what they call the "inner context", consisting of organizational structure, culture, strategy, and related aspects. This kind of framework is much broader than simply using need for leadership as a moderator and includes both moderators and mediators. It is perhaps more in the spirit of the earlier mentioned dissertation model, but is more macro and less micro. I mention it here to convey the flavour of how far some authors have gone in considering various kinds of contingencies for charismatic and transformational leadership.

CONCLUDING COMMENTARY

I now conclude with a few additional comments. First, it has been contended that leadership makes no difference (Pfeffer, 1977). However, I have argued earlier (Hunt, 1991) that that statement, though provocative, is not the point. The point is, "under what conditions (why, where, when, and how) does leadership make a difference"? The current article and De Vries' (1997) dissertation help us focus on the conditions under which charisma might make a difference—how much need for leadership among followers is there (why, when, where, and how), and how might that need be related to criteria.

Second, the article hints at the relational emphasis stressed in the recent Klein and House (1995) article. Such an emphasis focuses on the dynamic relationship across time between charisma and other variables. One of these could well be need for leadership.

Finally, as De Vries points out in his (1997) dissertation, a major contribution of need for leadership is to show what it *can* add to current work. In this he echoes the arguments of those such as Mook (1983) concerning lab studies—they show what can happen. I would simply modify this a bit by saying that for me a major contribution of the current study has been to show what might be. The "what might be" is suggested by much of my previous discussion. Need for leadership has stimulated it.

REFERENCES

Bass, B.M. (1990). Editorial: Transformational leaders are not necessarily participative. *Leadership Quarterly, 1*, vii.

Beer, M. (1966). *Leadership, employee needs, and motivation* (Monograph No. 129). Columbus, OH: Bureau of Business Research, Ohio State University.

Bryman, A. (1992). *Charisma and leadership in organizations*. London: Sage.

De Vries, R.E. (1997). *Need for leadership: A solution to empirical problems in situational theories of leadership*. Doctoral dissertation, Tilburg University. Enschede, The Netherlands: FEBO Print.

Edwards, J.R. (1994). The study of congruence in organizational behavior research: Critique and a proposed alternative. *Organizational Behavior and Human Decision Processes, 58*, 51–100 (erratum, *58*, 323–325).

Fleishman, E.A. (1973). Twenty years of consideration and structure. In E.A. Fleishman & J.G. Hunt (Eds.), *Current developments in the study of leadership*. Carbondale, IL: Southern Illinois University Press.

Foa, U.G. (1957). Relation of worker's expectations to satisfaction with his supervisor. *Personnel Psychology, 10*, 161–168.

Hemphill, J.K. (1957). Leader behavior associated with the administrative reputations of college departments. In R.M. Stogdill & A.E. Coons (Eds.), *Leadership behavior: Its description and measurement*. Columbus, OH: Bureau of Business Research, Ohio State University.

Hersey, P., & Blanchard, K.H. (1984). *The management of organizational behavior* (4th ed.). Englewood Cliffs, NJ: Prentice-Hall.

House, R.J. (1973). A path-goal theory of leader effectiveness. In E.A. Fleishman & J.G. Hunt (Eds.), *Current developments in the study of leadership*. Carbondale, IL: Southern Illinois University Press.

House, R.J. (1996). Path-goal theory of leadership: Lessons, legacy, and a reformulated theory. *Leadership Quarterly, 7*, 323–352.

House, R.J., Filley, A.C., & Gujarati, D.N. (1971). Leadership style, hierarchical influence, and the satisfaction of subordinate role expectation: A test of Likert's influence proposition. *Journal of Applied Psychology, 55*, 422–434.

Hunt, J.G. (1957). *Leadership and follower need satisfaction*. Unpublished manuscript, University of Illinois at Urbana Champaign.

Hunt, J.G. (1991). *Leadership: A new synthesis*. Newbury Park, CA: Sage.

Hunt, J.G. (1998). *Contributions of transformational and charismatic leadership to the leadership field: A historical perspective*. Working paper, Institute for Leadership Research, Texas Tech University, Lubbock, TX.

Hunt, J.G., & Boal, K.B. (1996). *Charismatic leadership: An experimental test of two forms of charisma*. Paper presented at the 1996 Western Academy of Management, Banff, Alberta Canada.

Hunt, J.G., Boal, K.B., & Dodge, G.E. (1997). *An empirical investigation of leader-centric and follower-centric approaches to charismatic leadership*. Paper presented at Work and Organization Research Centre, Tilburg University, The Netherlands.

Hunt, J.G., & Liebscher, V.K.C. (1973). Leadership preference, leadership behavior, and employee satisfaction. *Organizational Behavior and Human Performance, 9*, 59–77.

Kerr, S., & Jermier, J.M. (1978). Substitutes for leadership: Their meaning and measurement. *Organizational Behavior and Human Performance, 22*, 375–403.

Klein, K.G., & House, R.J. (1995). On fire: Charismatic leadership and levels of analysis. *Leadership Quarterly, 6*, 183–198.

Knickerbocker, I. (1948). Leadership: A conception and some implications. *Journal of Social Issues, 4*, 23–40.

Lowe, K.B., Kroeck, K.G., & Sivasubramaniam, N. (1996). Effectiveness correlates of transformational and transactional leadership: A meta-analytic review of the MLQ literature. *Leadership Quarterly, 7*, 385–425.

Mannheim, B.F., Rim, J.G., & Grinberg, G. (1967). Instrumental status of supervisors as related to workers' perceptions and expectations. *Human Relations, 20*, 387–397.

Martin, T.N., Schermerhorn, J.R., Jr., & Larson, L.L. (1989). Motivational consequences of a supportive work environment. In M.L. Maehr & C. Ames (Eds.), *Advances in motivation and achievement: Motivation enhancing environment* (Vol. 6, pp. 179–214). Greenwich, CT: JAI Press.

Meindl, J.R. (1990). On leadership: An alternative to the conventional wisdom. In B.M. Staw & L.L. Cummings (Eds.), *Research in organizational behavior, Vol. 12* (pp. 159–203). Greenwich, CT: JAI Press.

Meindl, J.R., & Ehrlich, S.B. (1988, May). *Developing a romance of leadership scale*. Paper presented at the meeting of the Eastern Academy of Management, Washington, DC.

Mook, D.G. (1983). In defense of external invalidity. *American Psychologist, 38*, 379–387.

Nealey, S.M., & Blood, M.R. (1968). Leadership performance of nursing supervisors at two organizational levels. *Journal of Applied Psychology, 52*, 414–422.

Pawar, B.S., & Eastman, K.K. (1997). The nature and implications of contextual influences on transformational leadership: A conceptual examination. *Academy of Management Review, 22*, 80–109.

Pfeffer, J. (1977). The ambiguity of leadership. *Academy of Management Review, 2*, 104–112.

Porter, L.W. (1962). Job attitudes in management: Pt. I. Perceived deficiencies in need fulfillment as a function of job level. *Journal of Applied Psychology, 46*, 375–384.

Schermerhorn, J.R., Jr., Hunt, J.G., & Osborn, R.N. (1991). *Managing organizational behavior* (4th ed.), New York: Wiley.

Wood, D.A. (1970). The feasibility of a discrepant approach in assessing job attitudes. *Organizational Behavior and Human Performance, 5*, 517–541.

Yukl, G. (1971). Toward a behavioral theory of leadership. *Organizational Behavior and Human Performance, 6*, 414–440.

Yukl, G. (1998). *Leadership in organizations* (4th ed.). Upper Saddle River, NJ: Prentice-Hall.

EUROPEAN JOURNAL OF WORK AND ORGANIZATIONAL PSYCHOLOGY, 1999, 8 (1), 135–138

Epilogue

Sandra G.L. Schruijer

*Work and Organization Research Centre, Tilburg University,
The Netherlands*

Leopold S. Vansina

*Professional Development Institute. Catholic University of Leuven
and Louvain-la-Neuve, Belgium*

The articles in this special issue covered a vast area of different approaches and methodologies. One picture clearly emerges from reading the various contributions: Leadership needs to be studied in relation to the changing realities of the organization. These realities have a direct influence on the tasks and the members that are an integral part of the social process of leadership. Organizations become more and more a changing constellation of diverse interest groups whose goals and expectations may conflict or converge. Mergers and acquisitions, subcontracting, co-makerships, preferential suppliers, and key customers are bringing in individuals and groups with different values and aspirations. Different classes of employees are being created in function of their strategic relevance. We talk about core-, non-core, and peripheral employees; about temporary workers and professionals. These people are exposed to different influences while working on different sites: in the factory, in the office, at home, or elsewhere. Furthermore, the leaders themselves move more rapidly from one position to another, in the same or to different organizations. From this perspective it may be more accurate to see leadership as: "a social process ... of dynamic collaboration, where individuals and organization members authorize themselves and others to interact in ways that experiment with new forms of intellectual and social meaning" (Gemmill & Oakley, 1992, p. 124). How does the assigned or created leader—through projected expectations—achieve collaboration for strategic objectives in the changing constellation of a diversity of interest groups? What is required to develop and maintain an organizational identity when the organization itself is composed of groups holding different

Requests for reprints should be addressed to S.G.L. Schruijer, Work and Organization Research Centre, Tilburg University, PO Box 90153, 5000 LE Tilburg, The Netherlands; email: s.g.l.schruijer@kub.nl loyalties and interests? When mobility in appointed leaders and employees result in increasing temporary relationships (see, for example, Shamir on leadership in "boundaryless" organizations, this issue)? When we take these organizational changes into account, we may better explore other domains of scientific inquiry for ideas about what the new leadership consists of, such as leadership in multi-party issues. These explorations need in our view to be realized from two major perspectives. The first perspective is gaining understanding of the nature of the *collaborative processes* that need to be "led" to generate co-ordinated actions. The second perspective is of a more practical nature. One needs to explore how persons in assigned or attributed leadership positions handle the projected leader-expectations to enable the collaborative processes to be shared within that system of diversity. What then are the required *capabilities and skills* of these kinds of persons in leadership positions?

The leader in the social processes just described may not be confined to one individual, although the person at a specific position may still be the object of projected leader-expectations and qualifications. In fact different persons may contribute to the crucial task of "leading" collaborative processes. But that may also be true for leadership in general. Often leadership is studied from the perspective of "the individual". Nevertheless, many decisions are taken by and in groups, in which individual roles may differ yet where the group itself feels and/or is responsible for the decisions taken. These groups could be top management teams, project groups, semi-autonomous work groups, etc. A formal leader or manager may have been appointed to the group, but the group can share various leadership functions (see e.g. Yukl on shared leadership, and, Shamir on dis-posable leadership and, collective leadership, this issue). A formal designated or appointed leader can in these situations rotate, and/or act more as a facilitator or co-ordinator. For self-managed teams to function effectively, several organ-izational conditions need to be fulfilled (Yukl, 1998), for instance concerning the nature of the organizational structure and its culture. Some argue that the leadership of CEOs needs to be less direct and more invisible by delegating, developing a community with a common purpose and shared values, and, by liberating the entrepreneurial energies of people, and so create conditions under which people will say "we did it ourselves" (Pinchot, 1996). Research which takes a follower-centred approach (see, for example, De Vries, Roe, & Taillieu on the need for leadership, this issue), and the (structural) relationship between leader and follower (see e.g. Rijsman and his reinterpretation of experiments on role-playing and attitude change, this issue) greatly contributes to further understanding of the dynamics of shared leadership. More research is needed to understand the conditions for and outcomes of distributed leadership; yet, the idea that leadership is more a *function* to be fulfilled rather than embedded within a role or within a person is appealing. It does mean that group and organizational processes become very important in understanding leadership and its outcomes.

When studying new roles of leaders, such as "conveners" or "leaders" of collaborative processes, and when addressing the functional aspects of leadership, the social embeddedness of leadership processes and outcomes, both within the social system itself and in its environment, needs to be taken into account. For instance, in multiparty collaboration, the processes within the parties, between the parties, and the larger sociopolitical and economic environment are relevant. For leadership in organizations, nations, or other parties, not only are the dynamics within these systems relevant, but also the macro-developments and phenomena in the environment.

It may sound like an open door, but when trying to understand leadership processes in their proper social context, other disciplines, besides psychology, may have a lot to offer. Within policy sciences for instance, much work is done on interactive decision making and its facilitation, both between and within parties or groups, within a more complex political environment, work that has relevance for the way psychologists study leadership and decision making. Policy scientists could benefit from a psychological perspective and psychologists could benefit from a more complete understanding of the complexities under which leadership and decision making are shaped. Likewise, we were impressed with the depth of understanding some historians can generate (see, for example, Bass on the relevance of psychohistory, this issue). A good example is the work by Kershaw (1993), who tackles complex questions concerning the power of Hitler, and, whether he should be considered as a "weak" or "strong" leader. By not only focusing on the individual and his personal style, but also integrating the needs and motives of followers and parties striving for power themselves, he offers intriguing and very nuanced insights. He shows that the extent of Hitler's power differed for different policy domains (e.g. domestic policy, foreign policy), and that (as well as how) it changed over time. Other disciplines, such as sociology or philosophy, may have interesting contributions to make too. It struck us that researchers in disciplines other than psychology often ask themselves comparable questions, in this case with respect to leadership.

Remaining informed about the progress made in different disciplines, let alone engaging in multidisciplinary or even interdisciplinary research, is a very difficult or perhaps impossible task. Already within disciplines a variety of approaches may exist. Within psychology, researchers working within personality psychology, social psychology, organizational psychology, and psychoanalysis (see, for example, Vansina and his observations and interpretations of the dynamics of leadership processes in strategic business unit management) do concern themselves with leadership issues. These researchers, moreover, may adopt different research philosophies and methodologies. All of these can contribute to a further understanding of leadership processes. We invite the reader to integrate such rich variety (so meaningful in the social sciences) in his or her own way, and hope that this special issue on Leadership and Organizational Change represents a modest attempt to enable the reader to do so.

REFERENCES

Gemmill, G., & Oakley, J. (1992). Leadership: An alienating social myth? *Human Relations*, *45*, 113–119.

Kershaw, I. (1993). *The Nazi dictatorship: Problems and perspectives of interpretation*. London: Arnold.

Pinchot, G. (1996). Creating organizations with many leaders. In F. Hesselbein, M. Goldsmith, & R. Beckhard (Eds.), *Leader of the future* (pp. 25–39). San Francisco: Jossey-Bass.

Yukl, G. (1998). *Leadership in organizations*. Upper Sadle River, NJ: Prentice-Hall.

THE EUROPEAN JOURNAL OF WORK AND ORGANIZATIONAL PSYCHOLOGY, 1999, *8*(1) 139–144

PROFESSIONAL NEWS SECTION
John Toplis, Editor

CONTENTS

Copy and information for the Professional News Section should be sent to: John Toplis, Employee Development Manager, Royal Mail Anglia, The Vineyards, Great Baddow, Chelmsford, Essex CM99 1AA.
Telephone 01245 243189; Fax 01245 243062;
Email: John.Toplis@btinternet.com
The Section Editor's views are not necessarily those of the British Post Office or of Royal Mail.

CAREER MANAGEMENT
John Toplis

In common with other large employers in the UK, Royal Mail recruits graduates in the belief that some are likely to be among the top managers of the future.

At the end of last year, we held a meeting for the graduates working in Royal Mail Anglia. One of the aims of the meeting was to advise them on how they might manage their careers, and to that end I prepared notes for them and for those who may advise them.

The notes for advisors follow. They may be of wider interest: I would also be interested in views about them.

1. Early in their career, people may get the chance to work in several different departments or functions over a short period of time. If the opportunity is offered, encourage them to take it for three reasons:

- it will give them a broad view of the organization;
- some of the people that they meet will form part of their personal network in the future;
- it will help people to decide where they want to start their career.

---

2. Encourage people to decide whether and where they are going to specialize in the early stages of their career. Their may well reflect their interests, their abilities and their circumstances. It may also reflect the wish to gain a professional qualification, or it may be that they want to take on a job that will help them to understand the organization better and to further build their 'network' of contacts. The former option could be the first step towards being a functional specialist; the latter could be a step towards general management.

3. Encourage people to find time to plan investment in themselves. It is important to have personal objectives and goals which will systematically develop work experience and potential; often these objectives and goals can be built into work objectives; they need not make great demands on life outside work.

4. If people want to get on, it is important that they focus on some specific measurable achievements which the organization is likely to value, and then work hard to achieve them. In contrast, people who do a lot of things but who don't do any of them to a really high standard may find it difficult to get on.

5. 'Getting on' can also depend on developing good skills at being interviewed and assessed. Although the integrity of a specific selection procedure must not be compromised, people should seek general information about the processes that they are facing. This is particularly important in some of the new competency based procedures in which assessors are looking for evidence of specific positive behaviours (and for the avoidance of negative indicators). Unless you have researched the positive behaviours required and gained the necessary experience, you are unlikely to be able to provide the assessor with the required information on the day of the assessment.

6. If there are setbacks at assessments, encourage people to learn from them. Assessors seldom change their mind about the outcome of assessments, but any if it is clear that people want to discuss how they can build on the experience and do better next time, they can be a valuable source of information. Successful candidates might be reminded that assessors can pass on tips about how they could do even better in the future.

7. After people have been with the organization some three to five years, the most able need to give further thought to the issue of whether they are going to be a functional specialist, a general manager, or some combination of the two. In order to decide, there are three things to take into account.
      (i) The first is what the different roles involve:

• Functional specialists tend to like details. Mastery of detail can help to give them confidence and authority. People may seek their advice and respect them because of their knowledge. In contrast, the same people can feel uncomfortable if they haven't sufficient time to work to professional standards;
• General managers tend to less concerned with fine detail and to focus more on high-level issues such as the direction of the organization, its competitors, its human and other resources, its processes and its profitability. General managers are more comfortable with imperfect information, relying on functional specialists to go into details when required;

• Many managers fall somewhere between these two extremes. For example, while some may gain experience of several different functions they may be attracted to detail and behave more like a functional specialist than a general manager. Others may take on the role of a functional manager, retaining and updating their professional skills but spending increasing amounts of time on management activities within the function.

(ii) The second thing to take into account is what someone is like as an individual. Some people love mastering detail, while others are at their happiest when thinking about 'blue skies' and 'white spaces'. Some are particularly skilled at leading others, while others prefer ideas and problem solving to working with others. Some people base their career decisions on a careful analysis of their strengths and on the things that they enjoy, rather than on apparent opportunities for promotion; for others, getting to the top is the thing that really matters, even though they may get less enjoyment from the content of the work that they do there.

(iii) The third thing to take into account is the extent to which the individual needs financial security. If it is possible that an individual will need to change employer (and jobs for life are very rare these days), a business or professional qualification may make it easier for them to find alternative employment or even to be self-employed.

8. Some people find job and career choice easy, but for others it is difficult. For example, some people may be bored by the things that they can do, but unable to cope with new things that interest them. Specialist help may be required.

9. Here are some ideas from research into careers; some of them are almost contradictory!
• people generally get on by exploiting their strengths;
• 'successes' are more important than 'failures'—but the size of the mistake can matter; also it is important to learn from mistakes and not to make the same mistake twice;
• some people hit a 'glass ceiling' by overusing their strengths and by being too narrow in their view; they find it difficult to stop doing the things that they really enjoy;
• other people hit a 'glass ceiling' because they fail to pay attention to 'career stoppers'—attributes that keep holding them back. Career stoppers may range from a lack of diplomacy when working with top managers, to making errors in presentations and reports. Most people are clearly told what they need to do in order to progress their career, but some people find it difficult to take the points on board or underestimate the importance of the feedback that they are given.

10. Successful top managers are often astute at realizing the skills and experiences that they need to get in order to get on. One very successful manager applied thirteen times for a kind of job for which he did not appear best suited. He did so because he judged that a lack of experience in the area would hold him back. His subsequent success suggests that his analysis was correct.

11. Encourage people to review their career in depth every 5 years or so—they will probably want to do so whenever there is a 0 or a 5 in their age! Self-assessment can be a useful aid to career planning, but people can mislead themselves. For example, their idea of a creative idea may be someone else's

idea of a routine improvement, and their perception of a successful project may not be shared by others using different criteria. What really matters is how people come across to others, not only in terms of their personality but also in terms of their areas of competence and the value that they can add. If people feel that their line manager is not giving them an accurate picture of their strengths and development needs, encourage them to seek advice from others in their 'network' or consider making contact with a mentor.

12. During their working life, most people are likely to have several phases when they are unhappy with the progress of their career. In such circumstances, encourage people to try to build a workload based on the things that they enjoy and do well. If they have a specialist background, encourage them to make use of the skills that they have developed. If they have become more of a generalist, encourage them to revisit some of their specialist skills. Encourage them to seek out people who have appreciated their work in the past and see if they might help find a way forward.

13. To reach the top of a large organization, people will probably need to (i) work in several different functions (ii) work in several different businesses, some growing, some contracting (iii) work both in headquarters and away from the centre (iv) work overseas (v) enjoy the continued support of at least one Director or very senior member of staff. Although job titles may not change much, people will need to invest as much time learning about management as a subject as they did on gaining professional qualifications early in their career. Unless people have exceptional ability, they will need to give a great deal of their life to their career if they aim to rise to the very top.

14. In their early days, the job content, the pay, the prospects and the social side of work may be the things that matter most to an individual. But as they get older and become a senior manager, their values may matter more to them. In part, this may reflect greater financial security, but it may also reflect the commitment required from senior managers; it is one thing to work long hours for an employer that you respect, and quite another to spend long hours at work for an organization that you do not believe in. Encourage individuals to take values into account in their career decisions, and encourage individuals to seek to influence them if they conflict with their commitment.

FORTHCOMING INTERNATIONAL CONFERENCES

Raising People Issues 4th Test User Conference
9–11 JUNE 1999
THE ROYAL HOTEL, SCARBOROUGH, UK
Information:
John Walker
The British Psychological Society
St Andrews House
48 Princess Road East
Leicester
LE1 7DR, UK
Telephone: + 44 (0) 1162 529 555
Email: conferences@bpd.org.uk

6th European Conference of Psychology
4–8 JULY 1999
ROME, ITALY
Information:
Congress Organizing Committee
c/o INPPA
via Arenula 16
00186 Rome
ITALY

5th European Conference of Psychological Assessment
25–29 AUGUST 1999
UNIVERSITY OF PATRAS, GREECE
Information:
Demetrious S. Alexopoulos
Section of Psychology
Department of Education
University of Patras
265 00 Patras
GREECE
Telephone: + 30 61 997 737
Fax: + 30 61 997 740
Email: dalexopl@upatras.gr

European Conference on Safety in the Modern Society
15–17 SEPTEMBER 1999
HELSINKI, FINLAND
Information:
Ms Kristiina Kulha
Finnish Institute of Occupational Health
Topeliuksenkatu 41 a A
FIN-00250
Helsinki
FINLAND
Telephone: + 358 9 47471
Fax: + 358 9 2413 804
Email: Kristiina.Kulha@occuphealth.fi

AIMS OF THE PROFESSIONAL NEWS SECTION
John Toplis

It is hoped to include the following in future issues:

- Appointments made; these will be "Top Appointments", such as University Chairs, or Head of Human Resources in major European organizations. will be welcome.
- Grants obtained.
- International conferences; as well as the dates of the conferences, closing dates for the submission of papers will be announced when available.
- News of networks; we hope that the newsletter will help with the formation and devleopment of networks.
- Legal issues; the implications of European law in the areas of recruitment, employment and industrial relations is likely to be of particular interest to readers.
- Research collaboration; many individuals and groups will want to initiate comparative research studies across a number of European countries and perhaps outside the EEC as well—the professional news section will give researchers an opportunity to make contact will each other.
- Reports of both "confirmatory" and "unsuccessful" research findings.
- The comparison of alternative methodologies.

In addition I propose to collect contributions for a series of special features; each issue will contain at least one special feature, aimed at giving an up-to-date picture of professional practice and current issues.
I should be grateful if readers and contributors could help in the following ways:

1. Please let me have your views about possible regular/special features.
2. Please send contributions; please add your fax number to your contribution as well as other information such as your name, address and telephone number. If possible please send files in ASCII on IBM-compatible disks as well as hard copy—it could save me a great deal of time if you have written a lengthy article. I will, of course, return the disk.
3. Please forward copies of this section to anyone who might be interested, and encourage them to contribute.

I very much look forward to receiving your views as to how the Professional News Section might develop. Above all, I look forward to receiving your contributions.